the complete guide to

gay & lesbian Weddings

the complete guide to
gay & lesbian Weddings

civil partnerships and all you need to know

jo webber and matt miles

foulsham
LONDON • NEW YORK • TORONTO • SYDNEY

foulsham

The Publishing House, Bennetts Close, Cippenham,
Slough, Berkshire, SL1 5AP, England

Foulsham books can be found in all good bookshops and direct
from www.foulsham.com

ISBN-13: 978-0-572-03274-6
ISBN-10: 0-572-03274-9

Copyright © 2006 W. Foulsham & Co. Ltd

Cover photographs © Hayley Lehmann

A CIP record for this book is available from the British Library

Printed in Great Britain by Creative Print and Design (Wales), Ebbw Vale

Contents

	Introduction	7
Chapter 1	Congratulations! It's Your Big Day	9
Chapter 2	Commitment	15
Chapter 3	The Legalities	26
Chapter 4	Just For You	41
Chapter 5	The Budget	47
Chapter 6	The Timetable	58
Chapter 7	The Stag and Hen Nights	67
Chapter 8	The Guests	77
Chapter 9	What To Wear	87
Chapter 10	The Ceremony	97
Chapter 11	The Party	103
Chapter 12	The Speeches	118
Chapter 13	Capturing Your Memories	128
Chapter 14	The Honeymoon	135
Chapter 15	Love Is All There Is	145
	Contacts and Further Information	148
	Index	156

Acknowledgements

Thank you to everyone at *g3 Magazine*, to Sally Jeffrey, my family and my girlfriend Gemma Willman.

Jo Webber

Introduction

Congratulations! You're joining the first wave of same-sex couples in the United Kingdom to become civil partners. It's uncharted territory, and while there has been plenty of newspaper coverage devoted to the debate over whether you should be 'allowed' the same rights that heterosexual couples enjoy (and a fair bit to David and Elton's wedding, too), this is the first gay and lesbian wedding guidebook to help prospective civil partners in the UK plan their big day.

Planning for your civil partnership or wedding – call it what you will – can seem about as attractive as scaling a mountain in a snowstorm. But don't panic! With a little help to guide you through the pathways, it's straightforward to plan and budget for the registry, ceremony and celebration of your civil partnership from today right through to your honeymoon.

The final section gives you pointers on where to go for further information and contact details for organisations mentioned in the book.

chapter 1

Congratulations!
It's Your Big Day

Though the advent of civil partnerships has seen a host of companies spring up offering gay wedding planning services, the majority of you will still be organising the entire event yourselves (hopefully with the help of family and friends!) in the same way that most conventional weddings are put together. Indeed, even those with cash to burn may find that they can create a more personalised ceremony by doing much of the legwork themselves, and this book will certainly be invaluable in helping you monitor the service you are receiving from any outside agencies.

However much of the work you decide to take on yourselves, we will help you keep a clear oversight of the whole process and make sure you don't slip up on the details. Throughout this book you will find easy-to-use checklists that let you both see the bigger picture *and* focus on the little things that make a difference. We'll also offer hints that might give you some inspiration, as well as sharing advice on dealing with some of the more complicated issues surrounding your wedding, from unsympathetic family members to setting commitment guidelines for your own relationship. Above all, this is a practical guide to help you manage what can seem a daunting task by breaking it down into manageable steps. Though much of the process mirrors that of heterosexual wedding planning, there are some key differences – and with them exciting opportunities to rewrite the rule book.

PARTNERSHIP PIONEERS
In essence, your civil partnership is the same deal as heterosexual marriage; you are committing to a long-term future with your partner, ensuring that your assets and rights are protected by law. However, there are also some significant differences. One of those key differences is that unlike heterosexual couples you will not be able to marry in a church, synagogue or mosque.

Though most Britons rarely set foot in places of worship, they are intrinsically linked with the romantic tradition of a wedding and certainly provide a profound backdrop to the ceremony. You'll have to get used to the fact that you will not have this environment for your civil partnership registration, though if you find a sympathetic place of worship you could hold some sort of ceremony there on the same day.

Of course, whether or not you are people of faith, you'll probably be pragmatic enough to shrug off this inequality, just as you've maintained a brave face through so many other injustices in your life as a member of a contentious minority. And anyway, the fact that you can't register your partnership in a place of worship gives you a chance to create your own highly individual day that avoids some of the rather tired traditions of conventional weddings. You may have to work a little bit harder, as many registry offices are not the most picturesque places on earth, but that could spur you on to think more creatively about what goes into your partnership ceremony. It should also be said that if you shop around you'll find some local authority registry rooms and assembly halls that are quite stunning and can be further enhanced with floral displays or other temporary decor, and there also many striking venues – ranging from manor houses to the London Eye – that are licensed for civil partnerships.

Civil partnerships are a blank page in the book, a chance to write a new chapter for society, and you are among the pioneers setting out into a brave new future. The overriding theme of this book is that it's your day and you can take it anywhere you want, provided the actual registration of your partnership takes place in a licensed venue. Whether you want to go low-key and minimal or high camp and fabulous, it's up to you. This book will give you the tools, advice and planning structure to make sure you can build towards a day you'll never forget for all the right reasons.

WHAT IS A CIVIL PARTNERSHIP?

A civil partnership is an entirely new legal relationship, exclusively designed for same-sex couples. The Government has sought to give civil partners parity of treatment with heterosexual spouses, as far as is possible, in the rights and responsibilities that flow from forming a civil partnership. When same-sex couples have their partnership registered they are granted a number of legal rights. The key rights are survivor pensions, recognition for immigration purposes, equal treatment for tax purposes (including inheritance tax) and protection from domestic violence. Civil partners are also exempt from testifying against each other in court, just like married couples, and they gain next of kin rights, which avoids any problems regarding hospital visiting rights. There are, however, some differences between civil partnership and marriage. For example, a civil partnership is formed when the second civil partner signs the relevant document, whereas a civil marriage is formed when the couple exchange spoken words. Opposite-sex couples can opt for a religious or civil marriage ceremony, whereas the formation of a civil partnership is an exclusively civil procedure.

TIMELINE: THE ROAD TO CIVIL PARTNERSHIPS IN BRITAIN

While 83 per cent of responses supported the principle of a civil partnership scheme, the Bill proposing that this become British law had a rough ride through parliament, particularly from Conservative peers, and this resulted in various amendments.

26 November 2003
In the Queen's Speech, the monarch announced the Government's proposal for the introduction of the civil registration scheme for same-sex partners. A passionate (and often highly prejudiced) debate was kick-started across the media as liberals and traditionalists argued for and against this historic proposal.

31 March 2004
The Labour Government published the Civil Partnership Bill.

22 April 2004
The Civil Partnership Bill had its second reading in the House of Lords. This was the first opportunity for the legislation to be debated.

May 2004
The Civil Partnership Bill went through the committee stage in the House of Lords where each clause was discussed. To read the committee debates on 10 May 2004, 12 May 2004, 13 May 2004, 17 May 2004 and 25 May 2004 go to www.publications.parliament.uk.

24 June 2004
The Civil Partnership Bill went through the report stage in the House of Lords.

1 July 2004

The Bill had its third reading in the House of Lords.

12 October 2004

The Civil Partnership Bill passed to the House of Commons and had its second reading. The Commons removed the amendment passed during the report stage at the House of Lords that would have extended the provisions of the Bill to family members and carers. This amendment, sponsored by Conservative peer Baroness O'Cathain but with unexpected support from the likes of human rights campaigner Peter Tatchell, would have forced the revision of hundreds of years of family law. Organisations including the Law Society and Carers UK agreed that this Bill was the wrong vehicle for such changes.

9 November 2004

A further attempt to extend the Civil Partnership Bill to family members, long-term friends and carers was made at the third reading in the Commons, but a large majority of MPs voted against it.

17 November 2004

The Civil Partnership Bill returned to the House of Lords for the consideration of Commons amendments. Another attempt was made to amend the Bill, but was voted down by 251 votes to 136. The Civil Partnership Bill was passed.

18 November 2004

The Civil Partnership Bill received Royal Assent. It took a year to implement the Civil Partnership Act. This was to enable all the necessary changes to be made and implemented, such as changes to the tax and benefits computer systems, forms to be amended and for registrars to be trained in the new procedures. Changes were made to the tax system in the 2005 Finance Bill, so civil partners would be treated as a married couple for inheritance tax purposes.

5 December 2005

This was the landmark day on which the first same-sex partners were able to give notice of their intention to become civil partners. This notice period, in which the legitimacy of both partners to be registered was checked by the registry office, meant that the first civil partnerships were to be registered in 14 days time. However, a few civil partnerships were registered due to extenuating circumstances, such as the imminent death of a terminally ill partner.

19 December 2005
The first civil partnership registrations took place in Northern Ireland, undeterred by protest from religious groups.

20 December 2005
The first civil partnership registrations in Scotland took place.

21 December 2005
The first civil partnership registrations in England and Wales took place.

LEGAL! BUT LOVED?

Civil partnerships are a major victory in the battle for gay and lesbian rights. With the age of consent equal for gays and heterosexuals, gay adoption sanctioned and now the opportunity for 'gay marriage' we have come a long way from the dark days that hung over us until so recently. But while the UK becomes more gay-friendly by the year, intolerance is still rife and many people, while accepting of same-sex love, aren't entirely comfortable with it. A long history of persecution and marginalisation has ghettoised the gay and lesbian communities and though we now have bright, open gay villages such as Canal Street in Manchester and Soho in London and a host of smaller versions throughout the country, there is still some sense of 'them' and 'us'. Among many gay men there is some bravado in being non-committal, while many straight people, particularly of older generations, are still uncomfortable with the sight of a same-sex kiss on a soap opera.

You and your partner may be lucky and have friends and family who don't just accept your decision to become civil partners but are over the moon about it, and are currently blitzing the high street in search of the ideal gift or perfect hat. But for a great many prospective civil partners there will be some thorny issues ahead – particularly from parents and relatives who are anything from ignorant and uncomfortable to down-right appalled at your behaviour. You might also find that some of your friends aren't fully in favour of your decision, perhaps feeling that you are throwing your freedom away or rushing in too fast. Above all, what matters is that you do what is right for you. This book is simply a tool to help you plan and implement your decisions, but we will also offer some helpful hints for diplomatically dealing with flashpoints.

WHAT ARE WE?

OK, so you're going to be civil partners. But it doesn't quite have the same ring to it as husband and wife, does it? You're not exactly going to tell the shop assistant that you'd better 'consult my civil partner' before buying the new three-piece suite. Plain old 'partner', complete with its twang of barn-dancing, is likely to be the standard term, but since you're the pioneers setting the benchmarks for the future you can feel free to innovate. You could be 'husbears', 'the women' or simply husbands and wives – it's up to you.

You might also be wondering what to call your ceremony. You could go for 'partnership ceremony', or 'registration' or you could call it your 'wedding' – perhaps the proudest sounding of the options. Then again, you might invent some entirely new term for the day that in 20 years' time will be the standard description used by everyone. This is a chance for you to generate and build your own traditions. But then again, you might just want the quietest registry office partnership ever. The most important thing is that you're happy together and doing things your way.

chapter 2

Commitment

Question: how do you get a gay man to run screaming for the hills?
Answer: mention the 'C word'.
Question: What do lesbians do on the second date?
Answer: Sign a joint-tenancy agreement.
OK, these are stereotypes but they're a good starting point for asking some
important questions of your relationship. Civil partnership is a big step and as
such we wouldn't recommend you go about it like Britney Spears in a Las
Vegas wedding shop. If you're reading this, the likelihood is that you're in a
strong relationship and with any luck neither of you has any doubts about
your future together. But the keys to a healthy, long-lasting partnership are
trust and communication, and it's always worth assessing the nuts and bolts of
your relationship, especially as you are constantly evolving and adapting. This
chapter is intended to help you evaluate your relationship and ensure you are
both travelling in the same direction.

ARE WE GETTING MARRIED?

A civil partnership is similar to a traditional heterosexual marriage,
bestowing legal rights and also moral responsibilities on couples. The
key difference between a civil partnership and marriage is that you
can't hold your ceremony in a church. The positive way of looking at
this is that it is another opportunity to rewrite the wedding rulebook
and celebrate your union in a unique way. But you might also want to
question whether you are both imagining a future together that
mirrors the traditional concept of marriage, growing together in a
home of harmonious monogamy.

Are you taking the first steps towards exchanging rings at your civil
partnership ceremony and at the same time promising faithfully never
to sleep with another person? Are you both picturing a future together
where you never take a holiday without the other, perhaps even never
wake-up without the other by your side? Are you considering living
together or can you both accept the idea of living apart? We are not for

a moment sneering at monogamous love here – simply suggesting that you're as open and frank with each other as possible about what kind of relationship you want. Everybody is different, and different couples stay together (and, yes, grow apart) in different ways. Monogamous wedlock is actually a relatively modern European concept that by no means applies to all of humanity. Divorce statistics reveal that it also does not work for a great many modern Europeans and perhaps the model needs a few honest, forward-thinking updates to work for you.

Moving too fast

For some, it may seem easy to say your versions of 'I do' when the likes of Elton and David have thrown themselves at warp speed to the nearest registry office. A combination of this sense of civil partnership gold rush and reading too many OK! magazine wedding specials may have you thinking this must be the right time for you also. But it might also be that once the party is over, and your friends suddenly stop calling because they don't want to interfere, you are left alone to grapple with the enormity of 'marriage'.

Understanding responsibility

Entering a legal partnership, like marriage, is a daunting task: a lottery of life with no guarantees and no one handing out instructions. It will differ from your no doubt extensive experience of dating or living with your partner because it is a legal contract involving a life-long commitment, depending upon a self knowledge and confidence that few of us feel we have. Even couples that have been together for years find it hard, because suddenly the rules have changed. Just as in heterosexual marriage, you will, at your civil partnership ceremony be asked whether you are prepared to support your partner in sickness and health, good times and bad. Are you? In absolute honesty, are you sure they'll be there for you?

Arguments

Arguments are inevitable at some time. Suddenly things that didn't matter start to matter, because you are cementing paving stones for the future. What you agree now will be relevant in 10 or 20 years' time. Everything has to be sorted out. Who does the washing up, whose parents you'll visit at Christmas and how often your partner can go out with his or her awful but cherished friends. Will one of you be prepared to take on the role of traditional wife cooking a meal every night? Or do you expect your partner to share this duty? This might sound petty, but the more these issues are discussed prior to your ceremony, the better chance you will have at success. It's often the build-up of petty squabbles that break a relationship.

The big questions

But you might also want to consider the bigger questions. Does either of you want to have kids? And if so, how – adoption, artificial insemination, surrogacy or natural impregnation? If one of you has a drunken shag with a work colleague in a toilet cubicle, do you want them to be honest and tell you? Will it mean it's over? If one of you has a long-term affair, what emotions would the other go through? Use the planning of your civil partnership as an excuse to debate these difficult issues honestly – and if you hear things you don't want to hear don't fly off the handle. If you've got this far, the chances are you can go a lot further together, but you might be surprised by how much you still have to learn about each other.

WHAT IS COMMITMENT?

Whatever structure a relationship takes, all rely on some form of commitment. A civil partnership cements that commitment, but what exactly is your commitment? Are you saying 'I will stand by you no matter what'; that 'I will catch you whenever you fall'? Or that you always want the best for each other, that you want to help each other grow? If a relationship is to stand a chance, people must make their own commitments between themselves about goals and expectations, as individuals and as partners or lovers.

Your commitment

Ask yourself the following five questions:

- Do you ever make commitments?
- If so, whom do you make them to?
- What does making a commitment mean to you?
- Do you honour the commitments you make?
- Do you expect others to honour their commitments?

If you find that you mainly make commitments to yourself, or that you make them to others but don't take them seriously, you may need to evaluate your decision to enter into a civil partnership. If you generally make commitments and honour them by doing your best to keep them, you're already streets ahead.

THE MODERN MEANING OF COMMITMENT

Unfortunately, commitments made by their partners nowadays don't always mean what they used to. When we talk about love and commitment, we are really talking about attaching to or connecting with people and things. We connect to ideals and beliefs, to families, circles of friends, co-workers and pets. However, when the connection is poor, it can make us feel truly miserable. The lack of meaningful connections or attachments in our lives causes loneliness and despair.

Making a commitment

When we make a commitment to another person, we are making the agreement to be present and available, physically, mentally and emotionally. This is a key issue when remembering the long-term implications of forging a civil partnership. You will make agreements with your partner by exercising your personal choice. You communicate directly about what you will do, how you will behave, what your partner can reasonably expect from you and what you are willing to be held accountable for.

What is accountability?

Being held accountable means accepting responsibility for the results of our choices, decisions and behaviour, rather than blaming others or external factors. Individuals who believe they are in charge of the quality and direction of their lives, rather than victims of circumstance, have the ability to move forward. They focus on solutions, not problems, and they move forward towards the goals and commitments of their shared vision and purpose, both as individuals and as a couple.

Successful commitments

Couples who have clarified their own personal values, and individual and joint goals have a stronger foundation from which to commit their agreements and achieve more consistent and satisfying results. Success is almost a certainty when both partners keep their agreements, and conversely couples are at risk if one person doesn't keep to his or her agreements.

Sharing goals

Besides agreeing to work on issues that are important to the both of you, it is important to recognise your differences, and make a commitment to respect these differences. A major part of your commitment to one another will be harbouring each other's interests and life aims. As legal partners, you both share a keen interest in each other's professional and financial goals for the future.

Being prepared

Although you have agreed and accepted each other's goals, think about what might happen if your partner does not reach them. Imagine a scenario in which your partner has been out of employment for a considerable amount of time; would you be willing and able to support them financially?

You are both human, so it is therefore possible for one or both of you to step outside the boundaries of what you see as acceptable at any given time. This doesn't mean the relationship is automatically over, unless one of you makes that decision on your own. That is why it is important to be prepared with your commitment for all possible eventualities.

Take a look at this scenario and think about your reactions honestly. Your partner develops a serious illness. The physical illness becomes so stressful to your relationship that it becomes destructive. What do you do?

• Stick to your word and commit. Seek alternative help, use whatever money you both have to improve the situation.
• Re-evaluate your relationship on the basis that caring for someone with this condition is not an option for you at this stage in your career/life.
• Separate, but still be a part of your partner's life. You might take on a carer's role, but seek emotional and physical companionship elsewhere.

There are no right or wrong answers. Be honest and frank and think about what you would feel if faced with this life situation in the next few years. Not being able to take on the task of looking after a loved one who is seriously ill does not make you a bad person.

This exercise is helpful in understanding the absolute idea of commitment. Talk with your partner about other scenarios that you might have problems with, such as them having a drunken one-night stand with somebody else, having a secret affair or getting into serious trouble with the law. Of course, you cannot predict your emotional responses to a real situation, but just thinking and talking about potential deal-breakers will help you be more sure of your feelings and the parameters of your relationship.

What will change?

For couples that have already been together for a considerable amount of time prior to their civil union, it might simply be a case of no change after the ceremony. But for many there is a high chance that your relationship will change. A civil partnership can create fear of change and, as with all fears, this can be destructive. Suddenly, by being involved in this partnership you are making decisions about your future together that will affect two people. So what was once your decision becomes a mutual one.

LIVING HELL OR HARMONY AT HOME?

If you and your partner already live together, there are unlikely to be any surprises once you officially become partners. You may also continue to live separately. But for those who have yet to live together, it is worth considering a few facts on cohabiting with your partner.

The good, the bad, the avoidable

You may decide to settle in together because you see it as the next natural step in your relationship. The problem is, you might not be ready for it. Only when it is too late will you realise you've moved too fast. The important thing to remember is that when you and your partner cohabit, you will ultimately see all the aspects of his or her personal life, not just the pretty side. On a more optimistic note, this living situation will bring you closer together. You may start to enjoy your partner's strange little habits as opposed to letting it get on your last nerve. It's the little things that make a relationship last the long run.

PREPARING TO LIVE TOGETHER

If you are not already living together, you should give some thought to how it will impact on your relationship. It is different, so don't go into it without thinking about it carefully and talking about how you will each react in this new domestic set-up.

Make it your own place

Remember that the furniture and design of the place should involve joint discussions. Learn to compromise, but don't allow yourself to be beaten on every decision.

Maintain your mystique

The idea here is for both of you to become comfortable with each other at a gradual pace. It is not wise to show all your good and bad qualities at once.

Share the responsibility

Splitting up the chores should be second choice to alternating the tasks, so that both of you get your hands dirty. This will in turn allow both of you to put equal amounts of effort into the whole process of housekeeping.

OPEN RELATIONSHIPS

A recent poll of the sexual activity of European nations showed that Britons were the most likely to be unfaithful to their partners. The results stated that eight out of ten women and six out of ten men admitted they had cheated on a long-term partner. Yet the deceit and dishonesty that goes hand-in-hand with infidelity is still one of the biggest causes of heartbreak and failure within a relationship. Does this mean that those 'forward thinkers' – or 'loose sluts', depending on your viewpoint – among the gay community who favour open relationships are on to something? With the introduction of civil partnerships, now might be the time to re-evaluate the age-old question: do open relationships work in the long term and what are the benefits and drawbacks?

Jealousy or paranoia?

The major fear in any relationship, but particularly an open relationship, is abandonment. If you allow other people to have sexual access to your partner you worry that they might steal him or her from you. One thing that you don't initially allow for either is the element of competition. You can worry that your partner is getting the far better end of the deal going off every night with someone new, while you're stuck at home with a Pot Noodle because you consider yourself less attractive. The amount of communication necessary to overcome these problems is greater than in a heterosexual relationship and can be draining.

What if you're already in one?

Boundaries aren't static; they may need to change over time. This requires both of you to acknowledge and continually review what you expect of each other as the relationship grows. For example, even if you had both initially wanted and agreed to an open relationship, a few years later one of you might find that you have changed your mind. That means revisiting the earlier, agreed commitment.

Negotiate

You can't demand boundaries in advance or impose them on your partner, since you don't have the right to be in charge of the other person. You have to negotiate with them. People who try to impose on their partner tend to have short-lived relationships. People want to be loved and cared for, not controlled or ordered. If you are already committed to an open-relationship, don't be afraid to bring up the option of change, now that you are to enter a civil partnership.

top tip for relationships

Open relationships thrive on honesty and flounder in secrecy.

COMMUNICATE

There is no magic formula that will guarantee a perfect relationship, but making sure that you and your partner are able to talk openly and honestly with each other could solve a lot of problems down the road. If you're already in a relationship that lacks communication, there is good news: anyone can learn good communication skills. There are books, courses, and counselling designed to help couples improve their relationships through better communication.

GO FORTH AND PIONEER!

As we said before, civil union for same-sex couples has no real tradition to speak of. Commitment, however, is a common thread that is essential to any legally recognised union. Above all, for a lasting commitment to your partner, you need to learn about and practise forgiveness, when your partner makes mistakes, is unfair or even hurtful. We all make mistakes. If we expect our partner to tolerate and accept our mistakes, we must also forgive out partner's mistakes. You are part of a momentous change in society and there isn't much of a script to help guide you, so there will undoubtedly be times when you slip up. Just remember that you're both learning the ropes.

top tips for a lasting and
committed civil partnership

Be sure. Many people pursue relationships as the solution to their problems, such as insecurity, loneliness, lust, lack of direction or bad self-image. These will not necessarily be solved by a civil partnership. In fact, the problems are often exacerbated.

- **Be yourself.** We build walls by assuming that we will be liked if we could only be different from what we are. We fear rejection, so we conform to what we suppose others prefer. Healthy partnerships are not built on images or masks, but rather on openness.
- **Be friends.** Seek friendship and wait for romance. Romance will grab you soon enough, but friendship requires careful development.
- **Be real.** Live in the reality of where a relationship is in its development, not in the fantasy of where you would like it to be.
- **Be happy.** Enjoy your relationship and resist the temptation to try constantly to discern where you are in it, and where your partner is. Live it day by day and try not to evaluate it too often.
- **Be patient.** Nothing good happens fast. Be prepared to wait for simple situations, such as your partner adjusting to the idea that he or she has just made a commitment for the rest of his or her life.
- **Be motivated.** Many people are in love with being in love. Think about what you put into the relationship, not what you want to get out of it.
- **Be free and let be.** Allow the element of freedom in a relationship. Don't entwine the other person in your demands and expectations. It's easy to smother the other person, rather than serving them.
- **Be communicative.** Develop many lines of communication with your partner, especially in the areas of dialogue, problem-solving, mutual interests, awareness of each other's daily living patterns and habits.
- **Be sexual.** Sexual expression is a powerful form of communication, but can also become a primary concern and difficult to control. Talk early and carefully within a relationship about your sexual needs.
- **Be open.** Be open about all aspects of your relationship with your partner.

YOUR COMPATIBILITY GUIDE CHECKLIST

This checklist is all about assessing your compatibility on key areas. You don't necessarily need to have the same vision and approach to all facets of your lives, but it is good to know where you stand and where you agree to disagree. Each partner should mark each area on a scale of 1–10 in private. Then compare your marks together. The more honest you are, the more valuable this will be as basis for building a strong relationship. Don't just write down what you think your partner will want to see; a bit of ego bruising now is better than a broken heart later. Try and see the funny side of your assessments and give practical reasons for your marks.

	Partner 1	Partner 2
Dedication to your career goals		
Your passion for a hobby or side venture		
Your own intelligence		
Your partner's social skills		
Your partner's personal hygiene and presentation		
Your partner's emotional intelligence and empathy		
Physical attraction for your partner		
Sex drive for your partner		
Your partner's sexual performance		
The importance you place on money		
Your desire for kids		
Your desire to party		

Celebrity wedding

Elizabeth Taylor went through seven husbands, one of whom, Richard Burton, she re-married to make eight weddings in total. Of course, you could take the view that a civil partnership is for life.

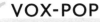

VOX-POP

Colin, 57, and Peter, 53, Stoke-on-Trent

'We've been together for 30 years. Coming together when we did things weren't easy. Public displays of affection were forbidden but we've managed to have a successful and monogamous relationship for all this time. Having said that, who knows if things would have been different in this generation ... there is a lot more choice, and commitment doesn't seem to be all that fashionable with the kids! Growing up when I did, marriage, or a union as we would call this now, is for life. My partner and I already know about commitment and our civil partnership just confirms it all on the legal side. It takes a lot of understanding, especially of expectations, but the most important thing I've found is to make sure your love is unconditional. I know whatever happens to my partner, I'll always be there by his side.'

chapter 3

The Legalities

It took much perseverance, persistence and belief, but finally the Civil Partnership Act took effect in England and Wales on 5 December 2005. Sir Elton John, Angela Eagle MP and novelist Sarah Waters are some of the more high-profile celebrities to give a thumbs up to the highly anticipated Act.

But what actually is civil partnership and how did it originate? Well, it is a completely new legal relationship, exclusively for same-sex couples and distinct from marriage. The Government has sought to give civil partners parity of treatment with spouses, as far as is possible, in the rights and responsibilities that flow from forming a civil partnership.

There are a small number of differences between civil partnership and marriage. For example, a civil partnership is formed when the second civil partner signs the relevant document, whereas a civil marriage is formed when the couple exchange spoken words. Opposite-sex couples can opt for a religious or civil marriage ceremony as they choose, whereas the formation of a civil partnership is an exclusively civil procedure.

 ## GAY MARRIAGE WORLDWIDE

With Britain finally waving the rainbow flag, which other places have also adopted similar legislature?

- Denmark from 1989
- Norway from 1996
- Sweden from 1996
- Iceland from 1996
- France from 1999
- Vermont, USA from 2000
- Germany from 2001
- Finland from 2002

- Luxembourg from 2004
- New Zealand from 2004
- Connecticut, USA from 2005
- Britain from 2005

Same-sex marriages are acknowledged in:
- Netherlands from 2001
- Belgium from 2003
- Massachusetts, USA from 2004
- Canada from 2005
- Spain from 2005

FREQUENTLY ASKED QUESTIONS ABOUT THE CIVIL PARTNERSHIP ACT

Of course, having the background to this pivotal and momentous Act is all well and good, but you need to know the core facts. Here is a comprehensive list of FAQs that will hopefully answer many of your queries. For further legal information, contact Stonewall or the Government's Women and Equality Unit.

What is civil partnership?

Civil partnership is a new legal relationship for lesbian and gay couples, aged 16 and over. It enables same-sex couples to gain legal recognition for their relationship. It is not marriage in the religious sense of the word, but gives lesbian and gay couples the same legal benefits and responsibilities as heterosexual married couples, just like a registry office wedding.

When did the new law come into effect?

The Civil Partnership Act came into effect on 5 December 2005, and as there is a 15-day notification period, the first partnerships were formed on 21 December 2005.

Why did we have to wait until December 2005?

The Civil Partnership Act required a large number of administrative and bureaucratic changes to take place before it could work in practice. These included changes to the tax and benefits computer systems and training for registrars who would be carrying out the ceremonies. There were also a large number of changes to the law that needed to be made, including pensions legislation, court rules and immigration rules; everything from the criteria for Jobseeker's Allowance through to the Explosive Substances Act 1883 was being revised to equalise the treatment of civil partners and spouses!

Why civil partnership and not marriage?
The rights and responsibilities of a civil partnership are ultimately the same as a heterosexual marriage. Civil partnership achieves parity with marriage in every respect, just with a different label.

How long do we need to have been a couple before we can do this?
There is no time limit to how long you have to have been together.

Is civil partnership available throughout the UK?
Yes. The Civil Partnership Act applies to England, Wales, Scotland and Northern Ireland.

What are the main advantages to registering our partnership?
Same-sex couples that register their partnership gain access to a number of legal rights. These include rights to survivor pensions, recognition for immigration purposes, equal treatment for tax purposes, including inheritance tax, and protection from domestic violence. They are also exempt from testifying against each other in court, just like married couples, and gain next of kin rights, which avoids any problems regarding hospital visiting rights.

Can I insure against being jilted?
No, you can't insure against failure of one party to show up on the day. But you can insure against many unforeseen circumstances.

What are the responsibilities?
If you register your partnership, you will be able to gain responsibility for each other's children, and will have a duty to provide reasonable maintenance for your partner and any children of the family. You will also be treated jointly for income-related benefits. This also applies to same-sex couples who are living together, but who have not registered their partnership, as with unmarried, cohabiting, heterosexual couples.

Do I have equal survivor pension rights as a civil partner?

As for widowers, civil partners can access survivor pensions in public service schemes and contracted-out pension schemes from 1988. For further details, contact the Government's Pension Service.

Do we have the same tax rights as married couples?

Civil partners are treated in the same way as spouses for tax purposes. These changes were dealt with in the Finance Act following the Budget of 16 March 2005. The tax office can answer specific queries about taxation law.

What about our benefits?

If you form a civil partnership, you are treated jointly for income-related benefits. This also applies to same-sex couples who are living together, but who have not registered their partnership, as with unmarried, cohabiting, heterosexual couples. For further information on how this may affect you, contact Jobcentre Plus.

What happens if my registered partner dies?

The surviving partner inherits in accordance with the rules of intestacy in the same way as spouses if there is no will. That person has the right to register the death of his or her partner and is eligible for bereavement benefits. He or she has the right to claim a survivor pension, has tenancy succession rights and can claim compensation for fatal accidents or criminal injuries. The surviving partner is also recognised under inheritance tax rules.

Should we still make a will?

As with marriage, you still need to make a will after registering your partnership, because any wills made beforehand become void. You will then be recognised under the intestacy rules, and will benefit from the same exemption from inheritance tax as married couples. If you have existing wills, you can either arrange for them to be amended before you register so they allow for the eventuality of a civil partnership, or you can simply have them amended afterwards. If you choose not to make a will, your civil partner will inherit under the rules governing intestate estates, which will take into account children from existing or previous relationships.

Do we need to be living together in order to register our partnership?

As with straight married couples, the answer is no.

Does it cost anything to register our partnership?

There are statutory fees, as there are for marriage. For further details contact your local council or registry office, or the General Register Office.

How do we go about registering our partnership?

Just as for straight couples, you need to go to the registration service to give formal notice in person of your intention to register your partnership. You will be able to register 15 days after giving this notice, during which time the registration service will check your eligibility. Following this, you form your civil partnership by signing a document in the presence of a registration officer and two witnesses.

My partner can't get to a registry office. What should we do?

There are special procedures for a couple in which one partner is either ill and not expected to recover, or is detained in prison or hospital. The General Register Office can tell you what steps you need to take to register.

Where can we register our partnership?

You can register your partnership in any premises licensed to carry out registrations, not just a registry office. For a list of licensed venues, contact your local authority, or the General Register Office.

Will I need a lawyer?

Not necessarily, but it's always worthwhile getting legal advice before entering into a civil partnership as you will become your partner's next of kin, and will have to have a divorce, should you wish to separate.

Does registration need to be local to where we live?

Couples can form their civil partnership in licensed premises anywhere in the UK, so if you want to do it with a local authority different from the one where you live, you can.

Can we have a ceremony?

The Civil Partnership Act does not require a ceremony to happen and it actually prevents any religious service from taking place during the registration process. Just as with marriage, couples can arrange a ceremony in addition to the registration procedure if they want, and local authorities have been encouraged to provide such ceremonies when asked.

How will our ceremony be worded?

If you do decide to have a ceremony, you should discuss what you want to say with the registrar. If the ceremony is being offered by the local authority, it will need to agree the content. There is now a standard form of words available from the General Register Office and local registrars, which you can use or adapt to your own needs, although the words themselves have no legal significance.

Will our details be made public when we give the notice of our intention to register our partnership?

Currently, if a heterosexual couple gives notice of their intention to marry, their details, including names, occupations and addresses, are made public, the marriage register being a public document. The Government recognised that there would be issues for some lesbian and gay couples, such as risk of harassment, should their sexual orientation be made known to the general public. Registrars therefore only publish names and occupations, and not addresses, to help protect people's privacy and safety.

My partner is from overseas. Can we register our partnership?

If your partner is subject to UK immigration control, there may be restrictions in terms of you forming a civil partnership. He or she might need to gain entry clearance in order to come to the UK and register your partnership. You will be treated just like a straight couple in similar circumstances. To find out how this may affect you, you should contact the Home Office Immigration and Nationality Directorate or the UK Lesbian and Gay Immigration Group.

Will I get a green card if I get hitched to someone from the USA?

The Federal Government of the United States of America, currently, does not recognise marriages or commitment ceremonies of any kind between same-sex couples. Therefore a commitment ceremony to a US citizen will not entitle you to a green card.

We registered our partnership overseas. Will we have to reregister over here?

For lesbian and gay couples that have already formed a legal relationship in another country, if that relationship meets the requirements of the Civil Partnership Act, they will not need to register in the UK as well. Schedule 20 of the Act sets out which overseas relationships are eligible. If your relationship is not recognised in Schedule 20, it may still meet the general conditions of the Act, which are in Chapter 2 of the Act.

What will we be called after we register our partnership?

Legally you will be civil partners. You can also take your partner's surname. Your civil partnership certificate, along with proof of identity, will enable you to change your name on your passport and on your driving licence.

Is there a divorce procedure if it doesn't work out?

The divorce procedure for civil partnerships will be called dissolution and will be a court-based process. You can only apply to the court to bring your partnership to an end after at least one year together. The partner applying for the partnership to be dissolved will have to satisfy the court that the relationship has irretrievably broken down. The court's decision will be based on one of these facts:

- Your partner's 'unreasonable behaviour'
- Separation for two years and with partner's consent to dissolution
- Separation for five years
- Your partner deserting you for at least two years

It will not be enough to say you are bored with the relationship or have fallen out of love.

Rights and responsibilities on dissolution will include fair arrangements for property division, residence arrangements and appropriate contact with children. This is the same as divorce for married couples.

Should I make a pre-civil partnership agreement?

As with pre-nuptial agreements that are used by some heterosexual couples, pre-civil partnership agreements are not binding in court if the partnership is dissolved. However, any such agreement will be a factor for courts to consider when making judgements in connection with the dissolution. The shorter the duration of the civil partnership, the more equal the partners and the absence of any children in the family, the more important such an agreement would be for courts making decisions on dissolution. If you want to explore the benefits for you in having a pre-civil partnership agreement, you should consult a specialist family solicitor who can help you frame your agreement so it has as much impact as possible.

Celebrity wedding

Sir Elton John and David Furnish got hitched at Windsor Guildhall, with eminent celebrities such as Liz Hurley, Cilla Black and Lulu in attendance. Very swanky!

How does civil partnership affect us as parents?

If you enter into a civil partnership with a person who has a child, you will become the step-parent. The biological parents remain the parents. Being a step-parent does not confer any particular legal rights, so if you wish to become a parent you must formally adopt the child. If you wish to have parental responsibility, you will have to be granted this either by the mother in the form prescribed or by order of the court.

Does a civil partner with parental responsibility automatically become a parent?

No. The civil partner of a natural parent is the child's step-parent. Having parental responsibility does not in itself make you a parent. In order for the civil partner to become a parent, he or she would have to adopt the child in accordance with the specified procedure.

Can the ceremony take place abroad?

Only if one of the partners is a citizen of that country or has lived there for a certain period of time, and if that country already has provision for same-sex weddings or commitment ceremonies. Two UK citizens would not be able to have a legally recognised ceremony in Amsterdam, for instance.

Celebrity wedding

Lesbian entertainer Rosie O'Donnell was appalled during the trial with her magazine that her partner Kelli was called to testify against her. Married spouses are protected from testifying against each other. Rosie said, 'We applied for spousal privilege and were denied it by the State. As a result, everything that I said to Kelli, every letter that I wrote her, every e-mail, every correspondence and conversation was entered into the record. After the trial, I am now and will forever be a total proponent of gay marriage.' So there you have it; yet another celebrity advocate!

JUDAISM AND CIVIL PARTNERSHIPS

As with many other religious denominations, Judaism has many different strands of the faith, which can be broadly grouped as the Liberal, Reform and Orthodox Jewish movements. Liberal Judaism was the first religious organisation in the UK to draw up a liturgy for same-sex commitment ceremonies. The liturgy, called *Covenant of Love, a Service of Commitment for Same-Sex Couples*, is a compendium of texts from which rabbis, and lesbian and gay couples, can choose material to construct a commitment ceremony.

Prior to the law coming into force, Liberal Judaism's Chief Executive Rabbi Danny Rich said, 'Liberal Judaism will be in a unique position to meet the needs of lesbian and gay people.' Brighton and Hove Progressive Synagogue's Rabbi Elizabeth Tikvah Sarah, who was part of the Rabbinic Working Party that devised the liturgy, said, 'The Civil Partnership Law is a historic milestone, granting legal status and recognition to lesbian and gay partnerships. Liberal Judaism champions justice, equality, compassion and inclusion; the new liturgy ensures that these values are put into practice as far as lesbian and gay Jews are concerned, by enabling lesbian and gay couples to celebrate their partnerships in a Jewish framework.'

The process of creating the liturgy began three years ago, following the adoption of a policy on same-sex commitment ceremonies by Liberal Judaism. Although some of the materials are devised from the Jewish marriage service, the aim is not simply to imitate a wedding, but also to create a ceremony, celebrating love within a committed and faithful partnership of two Jews.

Alongside the new booklet, Liberal Judaism produced a leaflet entitled *Lesbian and Gay Jews and Same-Sex Relationships*, explaining the movement's approach to lesbian and gay individuals and couples. Of the 31 rabbis who are currently full members of Liberal Judaism's Rabbinic Conference, four are lesbian and two are gay. However, the Orthodox Jewish movement, led by Chief Rabbi Sir Jonathan Sacks, said it would not be following suit. A spokesman said, 'There is no prospect of the mainstream Orthodox community permitting same-sex commitment or marriage ceremonies. Orthodox Jews are bound by biblical and rabbinic law, which only condones sexual relationships between a man and a woman who are married.' Indeed, the Chief Rabbi does not recognise the validity of the Liberal or Reform movements nor the marriages or conversions they perform.

For further information about Judaism and civil partnerships, see page 148.

CHRISTIANITY AND CIVIL PARTNERSHIPS

By and large, the Christian faith has been somewhat divided on the subject of civil partnership. A Church of England Bishop's Statement on 25 July 2005 did not bode well for an accepting and tolerant attitude towards civil partnership legislation. The statement reaffirmed the Church's teaching on both marriage and sexual intercourse: 'Sexual intercourse, as an expression of faithful intimacy, properly belongs within marriage exclusively.' Marriage, it stated, 'is a creation ordinance, a gift of God in creation and a means of his grace. Marriage, defined as a faithful, committed, permanent and legally sanctioned relationship between a man and a woman, is central to the stability and health of human society.'

However, there was strong opposition from the Lesbian and Gay Christians Movement (LGCM). After rebuking and condemning this official statement, spokesperson Reverend Richard Kirker, with the endorsement of the organisation, issued a new set of rules and regulations regarding civil partnership as follows:

> LGCM believes that the Church of England should be saying to those about to register their civil partnership:

> 1 We wish God's blessing on your commitment to each other and we pray God that, through your public commitment, your dedication to the loving service of others will be enhanced. We pray for your families as they unite, and for your children, your godchildren, and all those who depend on you both for support.

> 2 We seek your forgiveness for the abuse your relationship continues to receive from some who claim to be Christian.

> 3 For those of you who are priests, we assure you of our continued support as you embark on this public affirmation of your love and commitment to your partner. We pray that this public confirmation of your loving devotion will open new opportunities for ministry and mission.

> 4 We seek your assistance as we lead the church to a fuller Christian understanding of love, sex, commitment, partnership, marriage and the development and maintenance of family life.

> 5 We seek your co-operation in developing appropriate forms of public worship, which will encompass the public affirmation of your partnership.

The LGCM also offers a number of services of religious blessing. You can also find more support at Changing Attitude, which is a network of lesbian, gay, bisexual, transgender and heterosexual members of the Church of England.

ISLAM AND CIVIL PARTNERSHIPS

Although it is often difficult for many Muslims to be openly gay, there is one organisation able to offer help and support. Although the majority of faith members do not accept civil partnership and same-sex unions, Imaan is a social support network for lesbian, gay, bisexual and trans Muslims that has been operating since 1998. This is its official statement on civil partnerships, issued on 7 January 2006:

Bismillah A-Rahman A-Raheem

In the name of God, the most Merciful, the most Compassionate.

Imaan, the social support group for lesbian, gay, bisexual and trans Muslims welcomes the advent of the civil partnership in the UK.

Muslims view marriage as the foundation of society and family life. In a practical aspect, Islamic marriage is thus structured through legally enforceable rights and duties of both parties. In an atmosphere of love and respect, these rights and duties provide a framework for the balance of family life and the fulfilment of both partners.

And among His signs is this, that He created for you mates from among yourselves, that you may dwell in tranquillity with them, and He has put love and mercy between your hearts. Verily in that are signs for those who reflect. *Qur'an 30:21*

NAME CHANGE INFORMATION

There is no legal requirement for either one of the couple to change his or her surname upon entering into a civil partnership. However, there are a large percentage of couples that want to share the same surname.

There are two options available to the couple that do not require a deed poll, which mirror the traditional rights afforded to married couples:

- to continue using their names; or,
- one of the couple to change their surname to their partner's surname

If one of the couple wishes to change their surname to the other's surname, the civil partnership certificate provides the necessary documentary evidence of the change of surname. By sending the civil partnership certificate to all concerned, the person's documents and records will be changed to show the new surname.

If one half of the couple does not wish to take their partner's surname, the following options should be considered:

Double-barrelling your surnames

A double-barrelled surname uses both couples' surnames. The two elements of the new surname can be linked by a hyphen or kept separate e.g. John SMITH-JONES or John SMITH JONES. It is personal choice whether a hyphen is used and in which order the names are placed. However, most couples will find that one way sounds better than the other when the new surname is spoken.

Should either or both of the couple decide to have a double-barrelled surname, a deed poll is usually required. Although some companies and organisations will change their records to show a double-barrelled surname upon presentation of the civil partnership certificate, many will not, particularly the financial institutions (just as they require a deed poll to double-barrel the surnames of married couples). A deed poll will guarantee that everyone will accept the surname you choose without question. All government departments, including the Passport Office and DVLA, will accept a civil partnership certificate as documentary evidence of a change to a double-barrelled surname for both partners. The only way to find out if you need a deed poll is to contact everyone you deal with, for example, your bank, building society, credit card company and mortgage company, and ask what their policy is for double-barrelling surnames following a civil partnership. No doubt, in time, companies and organisations that currently do not allow double-barrelling using a civil partnership certificate will review their name change policy and follow the lead taken by the Government.

If you decide to apply for deed polls to double-barrel your surname, there are two options to consider in respect of the timing of your applications:

Apply in time for signing at your ceremony

If you wish to sign your deed poll documents at your ceremony, you should apply at least two weeks before your ceremony. You will need to provide the date of your ceremony, so that the documents can be dated before they are issued: so much better than hand writing the date when you sign your deed poll documents. Keep them safe until you are ready to let everyone know of your change of surname.

If both partners are changing their surname to a double-barrelled surname and deed polls are required, the cost of a second deed poll can be avoided if one partner changes to the double-barrelled surname before the ceremony. This must be done well before giving notice to a register office, so there is sufficient time to get all documents and records changed to the new double-barrelled surname. Consequently, the new double-barrelled surname will appear on the civil partnership certificate for one partner, thus enabling the other partner to use the certificate to get their surname changed to the double-barrelled surname without a deed poll.

Apply after your ceremony

If you do not wish to sign your deed polls at your ceremony, you can order your deed polls at any time following your ceremony. When your deed polls arrive, you can start the process of letting everyone know of your change of name.

Making one partner's surname a middle name for both partners

If a couple wishes to share the same surname but does not want a double-barrelled surname, one partner could take the surname of the other partner but both partners could make the dropped surname a middle name. Consequently, the dropped surname is not totally abandoned and a link to the dropped family name is preserved. For example, if John SMITH forms a civil partnership with Alan JONES and John takes Alan's surname, the couple could change their names to John Smith JONES and Alan Smith JONES. This can only be done by deed poll. The same timing considerations apply as discussed above. Because your names are changing by deed poll, you do not need to show your civil partnership certificate to anyone, only your deed poll document. When notifying everyone of your name change by deed poll, you simply need to mention your civil partnership so your marital status – civil partner – can also be updated on your records.

WHO TO INFORM ABOUT YOUR PARTNERSHIP

Here's a long but not necessarily exhaustive list of people to inform about your civil partnership. Obviously, some will only be relevant if you are changing your name.

- Employer
- Tax office

- Department of Heath and Social Security
- Local authority
- Doctor
- Dentist
- DVLA
- Passport office
- Bank
- Building society
- Credit card and store charge card companies
- Finance/loan companies
- Premium bond office
- Investment companies
- Companies that you have shares in
- Utility companies, including phone company
- Vet surgery
- Pension provider
- Insurance companies
- Mail order catalogue companies
- Motoring organisations
- Professional institutes and bodies
- Clubs/societies/associations
- Solicitors and financial advisers
- Internet service providers
- Magazine subscription

VOX-POP

Karen Johnson, 30, media professional

'I am fairly knowledgeable about the legal implications of civil partnerships, certainly more than my friends as I liaise with councils in my everyday job.'

Jessica Wilmot, 30, landscape architect

'I'm in the dark on a lot of the legal side although Karen keeps me informed. I would like to know a lot more about the financial benefits that you can get through a civil partnership.'

chapter 4

Just For You

Over the centuries, weddings have been renowned for exorbitant and often elaborate themes. Colourful costumes and distinctive décor are just two of the attributes that delineate what is known as a wedding theme. So, have you and your partner considered just what kind of celebration you want? Is there a particular scene or scenario that you have mulled over in the past? To kick-start your plan into action, you need to decide on your chosen venue, what kind of style and what type of reception you would like. By personalising the occasion, you can make the celebrations truly your own and set the blueprint for civil partnerships in the future.

By picking and choosing any marital traditions or organisational tips that have worked for other couples, you can have 100 per cent control of the way you want to celebrate your commitment. Or you might opt for something completely different and unusual. Many gay partnerships will have a totally different concept of what they want. The archetypal white wedding may not be applied to lesbians in the same way it is to heterosexual brides-to-be. Look at traditions and contemporary trends by browsing online or flicking through a few marriage-specific publications. Sit down with your partner and have a thorough brainstorm on inspirational themes and ideas. If this all sounds a little daunting, you always have the option of wedding planners if that suits you both.

GUIDELINES

There really are no rules on what a civil partnership should look or feel like. You are only limited by your own creativity and imagination; and the biggest pay-off is an event that it is completely representative of you and your partner. Themed civil partnerships tend to be more difficult to research because fewer people have the prerequisite expertise when it comes to planning one. There are many experts on *traditional* weddings, but only a small handful that are qualified to talk about planning a great *themed* wedding. Be prepared to get stuck in, delve deep and have your idea clearly and concisely in your mind or noted on paper. You also need to give your guests due warning if your theme is particularly daring or flamboyant, to give them time to prepare. If you do decide you want your guests to dress up for your theme, try to have some spare inexpensive outfits ready for those who might change their mind.

THEME IDEAS

Drag

OK, so it might sound a tad predictable, but we all know how some gay men like to don a pair of stilettos and lesbians love a little facial fuzz! Yes, this is a broad generalisation, but with gender play being all the rage at the moment, dressing up as the opposite sex remains a very popular and often amusing way to celebrate! We are all familiar with the concept of drag queens, from Ru Paul to gender-benders such as Eddy Izzard, Julian Clary and even Michael Jackson. Male-to-female masquerade has become an ordinary part of modern-day culture, and the drag king circuit (females dressing up as males) has also caught on, with a number of clubs and organisations catering for the trans community.

If you do plan to have a drag-themed ceremony or reception, be sure to mark this clearly on the invitation and be aware that some guests will feel more at ease than others.

Also consider that if you have a large catered event you might opt to hire out a troupe of drag performers to attend to your every need. Depending on numbers, there are companies that have regular performance artists to dazzle your glittering affair by sporting fantasy costumes and mile-high hair! Energetic and extrovert, these types of performances can often add instant life to your party and get your guests on the dance floor. Liaise closely with your drag performer(s) before the big day, especially if you are planning to have a very specific theme. Do you want to go for an Austin Powers psychedelic feel? Or maybe all pink to match your decor? Get passionate and let your creative juices run wild and free!

Many artists, whether working in a solo capacity or as part of a team, will offer cabaret performances, which can often rouse a lighthearted crowd. Other perks include simulating game shows, pretending to be celebrities, fire acts, dominatrix show and drag strip-a-grams, strictly for the over 18s.

Wassup Pussycat ceremony package

Is Britain too passé for your reception do? Legally speaking, a civil partnership must be conducted in Britain (see page 34), but who is to say where the reception can be held? For something truly outrageous and memorable, why not up the stakes and head over to the Gay Chapel of Las Vegas? You may chuckle, but this is Las Vegas's only gay-owned and operated ceremony chapel. It offers gay and lesbian couples a colourful array of ceremonies. Folks can have bespoke ceremonies or the chapel can cater to precise themes or ideas.

Our personal favourite is the Wassup Pussycat ceremony, with the talents of world-renowned Tom Jones impersonator, Harmik. This will surely be a once-in-a-lifetime ceremony! Harmik will perform three of your favourite Tom Jones selections for your entrance down the aisle and then conduct the commitment ceremony. He also sings during the lighting of the candle while you slow dance. Additionally, the package includes the use of the Tom Jones stage show chapel, theatrical lighting and fog among other equipment. Other hilarious options include live internet ceremonies and the Liberace and Gangster packages. Yes, it might be a little costly and difficult to organise, but for the truly dynamic and diva-esque this could be the perfect choice.

Celebrity wedding

Did you know that actress Pamela Anderson got married to Tommy Lee barefoot wearing a white bikini? They also got remarried for fun in silver space suits.

Ancient Rome

It can be jolly good fun to plan a themed occasion that focuses on a certain historical time period. The Ancient Romans were fond of purples, reds, gold and white, and wore more intricate and richly adorned clothing than the Greeks. They also began wearing the 'new' fabrics of cotton and silk (although silk was frowned upon). Jewellery was very popular and worn extensively. Togas were oval in shape and measured 5.5 m long x 1.7 m wide (18 ft x 5 ft 6 in).

For bridal attire, select a floor-length, sleeveless, toga-style dress, either in pure white or trimmed in purple, gold or red. Wrap gold braided cord to criss-cross the front of the bodice and bind around the waist like a belt. Allow the tied ends to hang down over one hip. Attach a sheer train to the back of the dress at the waist. Finish off with gold-coloured ankle-strapped flat sandals and a gold laurel wreath as a headpiece. Carry a bouquet of lilies, orchids, a single Italian crocus or herbs, which were thought to ward off evil spirits.

The groom should wear a floor-length tunic or toga, trimmed in gold, purple or red. Add Roman sandals or leather boots for footwear and a laurel wreath for a headpiece.

Escape to Camelot

Gather your family and friends around King Arthur's round table for a wedding set in the enchanting court of Camelot. This will require some planning, but if you get it right you're in for a wonderful fairytale, medieval castle theme.

Choose royal colours that are deep and rich, such as emerald green, royal blue, deep red, burgundy, rich purples, gold and silver.

top tip for stationery

Use calligraphy fonts on your invitations, wedding programmes and other wedding stationery.

Cotehardies were the preferred choice of dress for medieval brides. Attach a train to the back at the waist. Add a royal-coloured cape in crushed velvet, satin or other rich material, with or without a hood. The bride usually wore her hair loose, with a bejewelled crown on her head.

And for the groom? Get into a pair of tights, young man! If not, trim dark trousers will do the trick, with tall, leather boots. Add a knee-length, royal-coloured tunic, long cape and festooned crown. A sword belted around the waist and an arm shield with the family crest will complete the outfit.

Roaring '20s

For a quintessential 1920s wedding theme, think glittering lights, rough men and romance. Although known for its criminal age, the '20s also became known as the Jazz Age, with the likes of flappers and the Charleston. Music was upbeat and enjoyable, skirts were shorter and the economy had everyone in high spirits. This is the feel you want to incorporate into your theme.

Use lots of vibrant, jazzy colours to really illuminate the day. Brides should go for burlesque; something a little Marlene Dietrich-esque is sure to raise a few eyebrows! The dress should have an intermission hemline, making it shorter at the front and longer at the back. Dropped waistline and pleated skirts were also a popular look in the '20s. For the headdress, try a Juliet cap, coronet or a simple band of silk flowers worn lower on the forehead. Don't forget stockings that have noticeable seams!

Grooms should go for sharp suits, English driving caps, suspenders and wing-tip shoes. Most formal dress or costume shops have a great selection.

The big splash

How about holding your ceremony and reception on a beach, with an approved registrar in tow? As in the above suggestions, attire can be incorporated into the theme.

A bride could choose to adorn herself in a simple white dress, perhaps going barefoot or possibly donning a pair of Birkenstocks, always a popular choice. The groom could sport a casual linen suit, or shorts and a lightweight sports jacket. Again, go shoeless or wear 'Jesus sandals' or flip-flops.

Clothes aside, the decoration possibilities are limitless with this theme. One appropriate centrepiece plan is to fill glass bowls with sand and seashells. This simple idea is an excellent way to incorporate the theme into the decorations. Cover the tables with a blue tablecloth that is similar to the colour of the ocean and layer fishing nets over the table. Present guests with a collection of seashell-shaped soaps, which are relatively inexpensive and readily available. This idea will work best in the height of spring or summer, if you are keen to have blue skies; re-create a tropical paradise.

The London Eye

For something totally innovative and grandiose, why not pick a legendary landmark? Our personal favourite is the London Eye. With spectacular views and scintillating design, this remains one of the high points – quite literally – of London's landscape. If you wish to host your civil partnership here, you need to contact Southwark Council first to make a provisional booking and then confirm with the Superintendent Registrar that registration officers from the Lambeth Register Office will be available on that day at that time. Please note that it is essential that you agree the date and time with both the

Superintendent Registrar *and* the venue before making any other arrangements.

The ceremony is performed in a private capsule decorated with flowers. It is timed perfectly so that vows are exchanged at the top of the Eye. The couple are pronounced civil partners 135 m (444 ft) above London, surrounded by friends, family and breathtaking scenery. On the descent, the corks are popped and the party served with chilled champagne.

VOX-POP

Would you like your civil partnership to have any particular theme and why?

Sarah Humphries, 24, PR

'Yes, definitely, as it's a major life event, even bigger than a conventional straight wedding to some couples, as we've fought so hard for it for so long. And as you know, lesbians and gay men love any excuse to dress up! I'd pick an S&M theme because there is a large BDSM scene within the gay scene and for some it would seem very fitting to get 'hitched' in the state of dress (or undress) they feel the most comfortable with.'

Tania Poulos, 26, designer

'Everyone loves a party and this will be one of the biggest so any theme would be great: fancy dress in general, drag kings and queens, even sci-fi or movie themes. Bring it all on!'

chapter 5

The Budget

From funding careers in high NRG pop to keeping the world trade in Lycra vest tops buoyant, the pink pound – and its profligate spending – has a lot to answer for. Naturally, you will have exquisite taste and exercise sound judgement with your dosh, but it's not as if you get married every day and you may well be tempted to go on a spending spree. With the average cost of a traditional wedding in the UK being £17,000, it's no secret that getting hitched is bad for the bank balance. Overrunning by just 15 per cent will mean spending an extra £2,550 and the last thing you want is to start your relationship off in serious debt because you just had to hire that convoy of pink limousines and bullet-proof Humvees to transport your entourage to the registry office. This chapter is intended as a guide to help you make sound budgeting decisions that will allow you to have a memorable ceremony, reception and honeymoon, however you choose to interpret those wedding traditions. It should also be of use to penny-pinchers who have, up until now, never contemplated what kind of experience wedding guests expect when they receive that glittering invite.

TRADITIONAL DIFFERENCE

In terms of finances, the main difference between a wedding and a civil partnership is exactly who will pay for it. It was, until relatively recently, tradition for the father of the bride to pay for the wedding, which doesn't help either the men or women in this situation! These days, both sets of parents usually open their wallets, and the bride and groom often either pay for the wedding or contribute to the cost. Depending on your age and circumstances, your parents may not be around, or in a position to help with your wedding. For many gay people, relations with parents are markedly different to those that heterosexuals enjoy. Unfortunately, some parents may not want to attend your civil partnership ceremony or conversely you may not want your parents there. You need to work out who – from yourselves to friends and family – is in a position to contribute towards the wedding and how much cash you can raise before aligning that figure with your hopes for the big day.

TALKING ABOUT MONEY

Many people – especially the British – are reluctant to talk about money with those close to them. You may be lucky and find everyone from your partner to your parents initiates the discussion and sticks hefty lumps of cash on the table. On the other hand you may have to take the initiative. Firstly, work out how much money you and your partner can contribute as individuals. It's important that you're clear and comfortable about levels of finance. It may well be that one of you is wealthier than the other. This should not be a problem, but bad feeling can and will develop between you if you don't discuss openly from the beginning how much you're able to contribute and at what level you have to cap the spending.

As for parental support, if you both have a good relationship with your parents it will be worth asking for help. If they don't offer some financial support when you bring the subject of your civil partnership up, grit your teeth, take a deep breath and raise the subject yourself. Be positive and start by outlining how much you can contribute to the cost of the wedding. They'll probably want to know how much your other half's family is contributing. Be honest. If one partner's family is more likely to be protesting outside the town hall with 'God Hates Fags' placards than contributing a penny, make this clear to the other family, but don't milk it. If the bad news is that you really don't have a dream white wedding budget, be realistic and go back to your priorities. What's more important: a wedding worthy of a *Footballers' Wives* Christmas Special or the fact that you will be looking into your partner's eyes and saying, 'I will be there for you'? Remember how the romantic heroes and heroines of fairytales are usually the paupers not the pampered? This is all about celebrating your love, not getting into debt and creating unnecessary stress.

WHY BUDGET?

Unless you really do match the dream gay financial demographic and live among piles of pink pounds in a tastefully converted city centre power station, the chances are that you will have to plan the civil partnership celebrations very carefully financially. You should now know how much you are able to spend. An inherent danger with planning anything on the scale of a traditional wedding is that you can very easily over-extend yourselves, especially if you commit yourselves to expenses on a one-by-one basis, without keeping an eye on the overall picture.

FINANCING YOUR CEREMONY

The most sensible solution is to wait and save up for your ceremony plans. But with the wedding race having officially started, many of you will not be that patient in waiting. The average engagement in the UK is 15 months, in which time a lot of money can be saved. If this doesn't work or you can't even wait that long, you might consider a personal loan: the APR will probably be cheaper than loading up your credit card or using an overdraft, but, as with any financial purchase, shop around; it's likely that your high street bank's loan will be far more expensive than other mainstream lenders. If you are paying for your ceremony on credit, you should do what a lot of businesses do and defer paying the bulk of the cost until at least a week or two before the wedding, giving you more time to save. It's also important to be sure that those who have promised to contribute money towards your ceremony actually pay up on time. This can be a very sensitive subject for some, so it's best to have a clear strategy from the start. You may want to set up a bank account specifically for the wedding finances. This could be in your name or could be overseen by a parent or someone who is contributing the bulk of the money. Set deadlines for the promised contributions. Perhaps the best and most polite way to do this is to send a thank-you letter, perhaps with some flowers or a decent bottle of wine, to all those who have offered financial support. An alternative approach is for various contributors to pay for certain sections of the wedding. A parent might pay for the reception and party, for example, and a close friend the venue fees.

FINDING THE MONEY

Before thinking too much about what kind of day you want, work out how much money there will be to play with.

	Available now	Available one month before ceremony	Subtotal
Partner 1			
Partner 2			
Parent/Guardians 1			
Parent/Guardians 2			
Other family contributions			
Friends			
TOTAL AMOUNT			

 ## HOW TO BUDGET

The most obvious way to budget ruthlessly would be to go for the cheapest possible civil union price you can find (typically just under £100) and then build carefully upon that amount. Couples who get organised early and plan carefully are most likely to get a memorable ceremony at a price they can afford. It doesn't matter which style of ceremony you choose, you are at the risk of overspending. You should build a contingency of around 10% on top of your budget to pay for the 'must-haves' or last-minute emergencies you discover along the way. The key to budgeting is not finding every item along the way essential; a little imagination, planning and the support of friends and family can go a very long way.

Whatever innovative ideas you dream up for the day, it's likely to revolve around the official ceremony in a qualified venue and a reception of some sort with food and drink. On top of that, even a post-reception party and honeymoon may be luxuries. Civil partnerships are now big business for a newly sprung industry that sells everything from cake-topping, same-sex marzipan couples to horse-drawn carriages at an hourly rate, mark-up included. These companies are constantly looking for new and creative ways to wrest money from your wallet. Their know-how can be used to good effect by those with the money to pay for it, but you can create a beautiful and memorable day by doing it yourselves. If you do pay for outside help, always remember that the ceremony is for you and your partner, not the wedding company. If you so wish, you may skip all the traditions you like: cake, flowers, whatever. Once you've started your budget, prioritise. Keep your head screwed on and ask yourself honestly what is most important to you.

Haggle

Take full advantage of the fact that civil partnerships are a break from tradition: it can be any theme you want, especially if the theme doesn't cost much! No one will know why there is only one dead flower as a centrepiece and if anyone asks say it has always been 'our vision'. There is also nothing to stop you bargaining with your suppliers or asking for more reasonable options. Do you really need a cameraman, a soundman and an on-site editing suite? Or will just a photographer do?

 top tips for bargain hunting

Hide your excitement. Not showing your enthusiasm over an item that you have fallen head over heels with could be a money-saver. A company will be less likely to respond to a request for a discount if they feel that their product is your only choice.

Supply and demand. Establish how busy your supplier is around the date of your ceremony. At certain times of the year (specifically October to May), companies can be very quiet, so they will want your order as much as you want their products.

False impression. Give the impression that there are products from other companies you are seriously considering, but for a discount you are prepared to place an order now.

 ## COMPULSORY COSTS

For those of you intent on avoiding the lavish spending associated with a traditional ceremony, it is worth taking into account that there are set fees for giving notice to a civil partnership registrar and their attendance at a civil partnership registration. At the time this book went to press, they were as follows:

- Notice of civil partnership: £30.00 (each)
- Registration in the statutory registry office: On day of registration: £43.50 (£40.00 + £3.50 certificate)

- Registration at a Licensed Venue: Monday-Friday £260.00 + £3.50 certificate; Saturday £300.00 + £3.50 certificate; Sunday £375.00 + £3.50 certificate

You can only become civil partners at a venue that has been granted a licence to hold civil ceremonies. In this case your choice will be limited when looking for the most inexpensive route to go down, as all venues vary depending, for example, on the number of people permitted in each licensed room.

STICKING TO THE BUDGET

Once you've done your calculations and know how much money you have to play with, keep that in mind alongside lots of information on the costs of various suppliers and services. The sample budget sheets below can be personalised to suit your own needs. Use the quick-reference sheet for overall figures, so that you have a complete picture at a glance, and fill in the full details on the other pages.

- Go through each item in turn and obtain estimates or quotations. Write them on your budget sheet.
- Remember that an estimate is just that, whereas a quotation is a fixed price, although it will probably have a specified limit.
- Deal with reputable companies and check references if appropriate.
- If everything adds up to the budget figure, go ahead. If not, make adjustments and look to your cost allocation sheet for some potential money-saving tips. Remember what really matters to you and compromise on everything else. If nothing will do but having matching D&G ceremony suits (and whatever you guys want to wear), then compromise on the booze, the venue and the honeymoon.
- Once you are sure that you are happy with a particular supplier, check any contracts and confirm everything in writing to make sure your booking is guaranteed.
- Pay deposits on time to secure your bookings.
- Check that public liability and cancellations insurances are available.
- Allow yourself an unforeseen overspend margin of five per cent.

COST ALLOCATION SHEET

Item	Person responsible
Your outfit	
Flowers for the ceremony venue	
Flowers for the reception venue	
Partnership rings	
Transport to the venue	
Press announcements	
Photographer	
Videographer	
Register office expenses	
Reception venue	
Reception catering	
Reception drinks	
Musicians/entertainment	
Wedding cake	
Hen night	
Stag night	
Honeymoon	

QUICK-REFERENCE BUDGET SHEET

Item	Estimates/quotation
Ceremony venue	
Reception venue	
Catering	
Drinks	
Cake	
Musicians/entertainment	
Beauty treatments	
Outfits	
Flowers	
Rings	
Gifts	
Press announcements	
Stationery	
Photographs	
Video	
Transport	
Honeymoon	
Total	

BUDGET BREAKDOWN

Cost centre	Quotation	Deposit	Deposit paid	Balance	Balance due	Balance due
Ceremony venue						
Reception venue						
Catering						
Drinks						
Cake						
Musicians/entertainment						
Beauty treatments						
Outfits						
Flowers						
Rings						
Gifts						
Press announcements						
Stationery						
Photographs						
Video						
Transport						
Honeymoon						

Celebrity wedding

Who said celebrities were generous? Britney Spears and Kevin Federline made all their guests pay for their own drinks at their wedding party and served mini pizzas and hamburgers. Classy!

top tips for saving money

- Don't buy your clothes; consider renting your tuxedos or suits.
- Hold the reception at your home/flat or that of a relative with more space.
- Do not compare your ceremony to those in the press, and certainly not to Elton and David's.
- No account for taste. Keeping your ceremony simple will probably make it a more tasteful affair.
- Enlist friends and family over commercial wedding services. Use a friend's flashy car, ask your talented friend to make the invitations; you'll get a more personal feel.
- Keep beverage costs down. Serve punch and wine only or non-alcoholic drinks.
- Decide on a morning or afternoon ceremony and reception. Just as morning ceremonies tend to be cheaper than afternoon, so a breakfast or brunch is less expensive than a dinner. For an afternoon reception, serve cake and hors d'oeuvres, rather than a full meal.
- Reduce the size of your guest list; consider not inviting ex-lovers, work associates and casual acquaintances.
- Find a venue that will allow your own catering. This can save you hundreds of pounds. If it seems too stressful, then contact a local college or cheap catering staff to act as waiters.
- Have a buffet or barbecue instead of a sit-down meal, or maybe go for champagne and nibbles. Don't be afraid to ask your caterer to tailor the menu to your budget.
- Make sure that all quoted prices include VAT and are in writing so that you don't get a nasty shock after the big day.
- Check out chain stores such as BHS for great selections of waistcoats at very reasonable prices.
- Ask friends and relatives to help out with some of the costs instead of a present.
- Stick to seasonal flowers; they will be much cheaper.
- Send all thank-you cards via the internet.

VOX-POP

Phillip, 34, and Daniel, 27, Cardiff

'We did our ceremony on the cheap! We're just two normal guys who have been together for the last four years and had decided to tie the knot, so to speak. The whole point for us was to secure our plans together for the future that means having our mortgage together and other joint assets, making sure we're covered if, God forbid, anything happened to us.

'We knew we had to pay the flat rate for the ceremony, which only set us back about £100. We didn't bother with getting anything new for it, just smart clothes we already owned. Maybe if we had money to burn we would have gone mad for the hell of it, but doing things small scale really suited us anyway. My mum came and Dan's parents were there, then just a few close mates who all came to the ceremony. We had the reception in our local pub in Cardiff where of course everyone ended up buying us a drink to celebrate! If you've got it, spend it, but if not, do what we did. It's inexpensive and there's a lot less planning involved. No sweat!'

chapter 6

The Timetable

Careful planning and scheduling will enable you to truly enjoy every moment of your civil partnership. Arrangements for large formal occasions should begin at least six months in advance. However, if you and your partner are truly forward thinking, plans for the big day may even begin 18 months before. Here is a rough guide to timetabling a civil partnership. Please note that this is only a rough guide collated from a number of sources, but it should provide a good starting point.

SIX MONTHS TO GO

- Announce your decision to both sets of parents. It may not be a good idea to do this at the same time, depending on family circumstances.
- Arrange for your parents to meet. Again, this may be problematic, but maintaining strong relations with the in-laws can be advisable.
- Discuss specifics and payment with your partner and parents. Marital budgets usually play a very important part in any lifelong union, so start by having a preliminary think about how payments are going to be allocated.
- Make a list of those to be informed. Make sure your mum isn't the last to know; she won't be best pleased!
- Tell relatives and close friends. Only you and your prospective spouse will know just who needs to be told first, but avoid handbags and bitchy comments and tell your best mate before a throwaway acquaintance.
- Arrange an engagement party. Want a big bash to celebrate your civil partnership? It's your choice, but if the answer is yes, get planning as soon as possible.
- Decide how many guests to invite to the civil partnership. It's all about compromise. You might want a big, ritzy ceremony, whereas your partner might want a small, intimate affair, so reach a happy medium and celebrate.

- Consult both sets of parents about the guest list. If both sets are going to be involved, it may be worth drawing up a preliminary list to get a vague idea of numbers and seating arrangements.
- Draft your budget. This may be a little pre-emptive, but getting a loose idea of fundamental expenditure might be useful when it comes closer to pinpoint planning (see page 50).
- Decide on the type of civil partnership. Ever wanted to be Cinderella at the ball or Robin Hood in Sherwood Forest? Let your imagination run riot if you decide to have a themed ceremony (see page 42).
- Choose and book the registry office and provide details. It might be a good idea to check out the website of your local council to see how gay-friendly your constituency is.
- Provide statements that there are no legal reasons why the marriage shouldn't take place. These are useful if you are concerned about any external interference from a former lover.
- Obtain the registrar's certificate and/or licence. You will need to make sure that your designated register is able to perform a civil partnership.
- Choose and book the date and location for the ceremony by applying to the registrar. Get in there first and avoid disappointment by booking early to get the perfect date. Don't delay!
- Meet the registrar to discuss and finalise details. If you want a tailor-made ceremony, talk to the head honcho to make sure the ceremony goes without a hitch.
- Sign the civil partnership register in your locality. There will be a 15-day waiting period once notice of intention to register has been given before the formation can take place, so sign up early just in case.
- Choose and book your reception venue, caterers, bar and drink supplier (see page 108). Vol-au vents and triangle sandwiches don't cut it for you? Call Gordon Ramsay now, before he gets too hot 'n' bothered in the kitchen!
- Choose and order or make the cake (see page 110). There's nothing like a good old-fashioned layer cake to get the party started. So plug in, make a wish and satiate your appetite in the process. Yummy.
- Visit the reception venue with your partner to check arrangements. Want the works? From fairytale castle to fairground, London Eye to London Dungeon, make your wishes come true, but check them out first.

- Select and appoint any attendants who will perform specific duties. Want a best man or matron of honour? It may be a heterosexual tradition, but if you fancy having bridesmaids or page boys, then let them know as soon as possible.
- Discuss civil partnership plans with your partner and attendants. Once you know who is going to perform which specified duties, get together over an informal drink to have a chinwag about everyone's roles.
- Write thank-you letters for gifts as they arrive. Whether a pair of socks or a new kettle, chances are your nearest and dearest are going to want to show you how much they care, so pens poised.
- Choose and book a photographer and/or videographer. Want to archive those classic moments when your loved ones indulge a little too heavily in champagne and embarrass you? Of course you do; just ensure the photographer is sober!
- Choose and book transport. As much as we love the Tube, it may not be the best effective way to get your wedding. Horse-drawn carriage or Reliant Robin, punctuality is key.
- Choose and book entertainment. Four Poofs and a Piano might have a window, but you need to get on to their agent now! Have a chat with your partner to establish what form of entertainment will work best.
- Check and arrange passports. You'll need these if you're going abroad after your ceremony.
- Arrange and book your honeymoon (see page 135). From Sitges to St Lucia, the premise of a gay honeymoon needn't be any different from a heterosexual marriage. Find a good gay-friendly travel agency to book with. Check when you book if and when you need any inoculations. Contact your GP to arrange these.
- Begin any long-term beauty treatments. Now, we're not suggesting you get a drastic facelift, but if you want to look good on your big day consider starting any major beauty/health regimes.

FOUR MONTHS TO GO

- Choose and purchase your going-away and honeymoon clothes. Sandals or skis, don't end up packing on your stag/hen night.
- Choose and purchase your clothes for the ceremony. What are you going to wear? There won't be many couples that have not given that some thought, so grab a trolley, some honest pals and get shopping!

- Select and purchase the attendants' attire in consultation with them. As much as your sister may relish the prospect of being squeezed into a fluffy pink meringue, spare her blushes and consult her before deciding on her outfit.
- Choose and book the florist, order flowers and arrange collection/delivery dates. Flowers aren't compulsory, but might add a romantic touch to proceedings. Do some flower research before deciding on your chosen bloom.
- Choose and order stationery. Experiment with fonts. Arial black or gothic italics, the civil partnership invitation may be the first point of contact for your guests, so spell their names correctly and double-check addresses. Don't send them out yet, though (see below).
- Ensure that the mothers have selected their outfits. If both mothers will be present at the civil partnership, avoid faffing by organising their outfits as soon as possible.
- Acquire furnishings for your new home. If you're already cohabiting this might not apply, but for those newlyweds who have invested in a new home, it's out with the old and in with the new upholstery.
- Check your budget. With the event only four months away, now is the time to start pinning down how much everything will cost and doing your sums. Stay ahead of the game.
- Pay for the honeymoon and any additional holiday costs. With your dream location already negotiated and booked, having something to look forward to after the ceremony will add a little extra sunshine to the occasion.

TWO MONTHS TO GO

- Choose and buy a gift for each attendant. Of course, you may have a small affair, so this will be unnecessary. However, it would be a good idea to reward those nearest and dearest to you both.
- Acquire the wedding rings, with or without your partner. As an outward symbol of your love together, a ring is an important gesture to both parties, so take some time and invest in bespoke jewellery that suits you both.
- Arrange and pay for transport to and from the wedding venue. Organise this now to avoid any traumatic complications on the day.
- Send out the invitations. Check and double-check addresses, postal and e-mail, and phone numbers to ensure you don't forget anyone. Give a clear RSVP date for about a month before the day.

- Send/circulate your gift wish list to the guests. Is this a little presumptuous? Quite possibly, but if you don't want the same washing machine twice it may be worth hinting/telling people exactly what you'd like.
- Practise make-up. This is applicable to lipstick lesbians and queens alike. That luminous green mascara hiding in your drawer might be best suited to a Halloween party, so have a trial run.
- Decide on your hairstyle and book the hairdresser for the day before the ceremony. The Hoxton Fin is so last year, chaps! Take a look at yourself at the mirror and reassess the barnet. Surprise your partner with something new and exciting.
- Discuss and finalise photography arrangements. Whether your friend is bringing a digi-cam or you're using professionals, have a chat with them so that they know exactly what type of shots you would both like (see page 128).
- Arrange overnight accommodation and transport for guests if required. Whether you send your guests the website address for a nearby hotel or arrange their limo, make sure your guests will be comfortable after the ceremony is over.
- Write thank-you letters for gifts as they arrive. Don't upset your generous guests; whether large or small presents, remember to say thank you.
- See your GP/family organisation if you're planning to start a family. If you and your partner are planning to adopt or have children of your own, have a provisional appointment(s) with relevant parties to get the ball rolling.
- See your GP/dentist/optician/medical consultant. If you and/or your partner have health problems, make sure you have your condition under control well before the big day. If you're on regular medication, check you have enough to see you through until you return from your honeymoon.
- Arrange insurance against cancellation of the wedding and loss of/damage to attire/gifts. This may sound a little pessimistic, but if something does go wrong on the big day, ensure that you will receive some recompense.
- Pay for the flowers. Flowers remain an integral part of any happy occasion, so maintain a good rapport with the florist and have a bloomin' good celebration!
- Write your speech for the reception (see page 118). Whether it's you or your partner that will be making a reception speech, now is the time to start considering the framework.

ONE MONTH TO GO

- Arrange a fitting session for your clothes and those of your attendants. A dodgy hemline or an unflattering waistline bulge needn't be an option on your wedding day. Check your attire now to make sure you are looking your best.

- Finalise rehearsal arrangements with the civil partnership party. Most couples will want to have a run-through of proceedings to calm nerves and correct any last-minute complications.

- Arrange pre-wedding parties. Hen night? Stag do? Want to give it another name? Embrace your final night of 'freedom' and organise a shindig with your closest pals. Just watch out for that stripper (see page 67)!

- Confirm guest numbers for the reception. Time to pin down those numbers, so compiling a simple tick box checklist of who's accepted might aid the cause (see page 80).

- Confirm all appointments and arrangements with suppliers. However grand or intimate your ceremony, make sure everything is in place. Again, a straightforward tick box checklist might be an asset.

- Order currency or travellers cheques for your honeymoon. It's so easy now with euros if you're travelling close to home, so get it sorted ready to splash out on your partner as soon as you hit your romantic spot.

- Inform organisations of impending name change and new address, if relevant. You may/not choose to adopt your partner's surname but keep significant organisations informed of any major changes (see page 39).

- Prepare and submit any announcements to the press. Not only for the rich and famous, but also for regional/national press listings.

- Book the hairdresser/beauty therapist for the day before the wedding. Whether you're male or female, the chances are you'll be preparing to get yourself glammed up for the occasion, so push the boat out.

- Confirm details for your stag/hen nights. If you're having a pre-civil partnership do, make sure you know exactly who is coming, even if you don't know what to expect!

- Buy ribbons for the wedding cars. If you're travelling on four wheels, consult the florist for a suitable bunch to adorn the vehicle of your choice.

TWO WEEKS TO GO

- Devise a seating plan for the reception (see page 107) and organise place cards for the tables (see page 85). Family rifts at the main table do not make for a pleasant afternoon, so consult your partner and play 'musical chairs' to ensure that there is no tension on the day.
- Give final numbers and seating arrangements to the caterer. Self-explanatory really: time to finalise those last-minute details.

ONE WEEK TO GO

- Wrap gifts for your partner and your partner's attendants. Store them away safely.
- Attend a ceremony rehearsal and hold rehearsal party for attendants, at which you can give and receive gifts. It is customary to pass on gifts before the ceremony, but presents can be given at any point you deem appropriate.
- Double-check arrangements with all attendants. Ensure that all parties know when and where they should be at each venue.
- Ensure that the speech readers' know whom to thank in their speeches. You don't want anyone getting miffed or upset, so make sure you thank everyone who has helped during the build-up to the big day.
- Attend and enjoy hen/stag parties. Watch out for that hangover; you don't want it to ruin your complexion!
- Arrange for gifts to be displayed. If presents are not going to be viewed on the wedding day, let people have a look at what you have received prior to the civil partnership.
- Practise your make-up and hair with clothes and accessories. This is probably more relevant to glamorous brides, but with your beauty regime already well underway, make sure all your attire is colour co-ordinated and ready-to-wear.
- Wear in wedding shoes. This might be more applicable to stilettos and high-heeled shoes, but if you're not wearing comfortable Birkenstocks make sure you don't have a nasty fall on the day.
- Confirm transport arrangements. Double-check that drivers are ready and fully aware of plans.
- Confirm final arrangements for the reception. Confirm the venue and caterer arrangements, including cake collection/delivery and the flowers.
- Confirm entertainment arrangements. Whether it's karaoke or

cabaret, make sure the performers are aware of what time and where they need to be.

- Pack for your honeymoon. Check your documents – and don't forget your toothbrush.
- Allocate any extra jobs to others on your wedding day. Don't run for the aspirin: you won't need to.
- Arrange for the return of any hired items for after the event. Check return dates; don't risk incurring fines.
- Inform the primary attendant when to collect buttonholes and to remember the rings. Depending on the type of service, reassure the best man/matron of honour on the order of proceedings.
- Appoint someone to make sure that younger attendants, such as page boys, are looked after. Let the adults have tantrums, not the kids!
- Go through the guest list with both sets of parents so they are familiar with names. If both sides of the family attend, do your best to make sure there aren't any uncomfortable silences.
- Pay bills that are due during your honeymoon. You don't want to come home to a pile of final demands!
- Ask a trusted neighbour to take care of the house/car/cat while you are away. You'll be able to relax more if you know someone is keeping an eye on things for you.

ONE DAY TO GO

- Visit your hairdresser/beauty therapist. Feel beautiful and radiant!
- Prepare your civil partnership outfit. Iron and hang up if necessary.
- Take a few deep breaths and relax. Easier said than done.
- Have an early night. Try to get as much sleep as you can. It will lighten any dark circles and reinvigorate you.

THE BIG DAY

- Ensure that going-away outfits and honeymoon luggage are at the reception venue. Travelling economy class in a wedding dress may not be the most comfortable!
- Take your going-away car to the reception. You might even be able to do this the night before.
- Give venue fees, if necessary, and rings to the best man or matron of honour.

- Arrive at the registry office with your primary attendant 20 minutes early. You and your partner will have to decide who arrives at the venue first to avoid any unexpected meetings.
- Check entry in register.
- Meet the registrar to have an informal chat. He or she should introduce him/herself before proceedings begin.
- Wait for your partner at the designated place. The registrar should be able to direct you to the correct location where you should meet your partner.
- Sign the civil register. This is a legal requirement. Place the ring on the third finger of the left hand, when prompted!
- Lead the recessional with your partner. This basically relates to who leaves the venue and in what order, and is more relevant to a traditional wedding.

AFTER THE HONEYMOON

- Write outstanding letters of thanks, including to both sets of parents. If both families attended the event, be sure to thank them accordingly.
- Order photographs. If you have had your pictures professionally taken, make sure that copies and any additional sets of photos or videos are on the way to relive your magical moments.
- Ensure that all hired attire has been returned. Don't incur any fines for lateness.
- Make sure any attendants have been paid for additional expenses on the day. Whether you incurred a flat tyre or needed an emergency pair of tights, make sure you reimburse those who helped you through the day.
- Arrange a press report. Make sure the publication you want gets full access to your wedding snaps.
- Entertain both sets of parents and attendants. In a good natured way if possible.
- Change all necessary documentation to reflect your 'married' status. A civil partnership is a legally binding contract, so make sure your personal details reflect this (see page 39).
- Review insurance provisions including life, property, contents, medical and car. As civil partners, find out which companies have the most inclusive, gay-friendly competitive rates.

chapter 7

The Stag and Hen Nights

The majority of gay and lesbian people in the UK are no strangers to pubs and clubs, proudly doing their bit to strengthen the stereotype of being the life, soul and corroded liver of the party. Indeed, there is this mythical suggestion that people who fall in love with their own sex are somehow the most sophisticated creatures that have ever prowled the night. And perhaps there's a smidgen of truth in that as we have, so far, gone largely untainted by that heterosexual rite of passage, the stag or hen night. Yes, although our social whirl may in reality be more Canal Street than Cabaret, the majority of us have avoided tearing down the curry house, singing football songs in a lap-dancing club before being tied naked to a lamppost. And as for the men…

Just as your civil partnership is all about you, so you have every opportunity to rewrite the rule-book when it comes to the stag or hen night. Since it's likely that you share mutual friends of both genders there's a good chance that, like Elton and David, you'll want to spend the night together. You might also want to rewrite the name for your interpretation of the tradition. One young couple, spoken to during the research of this book, marked their pre-marital blow-out with a 'Hag Night' in which all members of the party made themselves look as hideously unrecognisable as possible, a kind of grotesque version of a masked ball. Many will seek a more sophisticated way to mark the occasion – perhaps a weekend away with treasured friends – while others might base the event around cleansing mind, body and soul at a spa retreat. Whatever you do, this is an event to be creative with and to enjoy, even if you don't necessarily remember it!

WHAT TYPE OF STAG/HEN?

Depending what floats your boat, you will no doubt have different ideas of what constitutes an ideal stag/hen night. Perhaps if you are the slightly more mature gay couple you would prefer a quiet relaxing night in alone together, or if you're young and irresponsible a chaotic night out down Canal Street. Either way, discuss this and decide early exactly what type of stag/hen do you are aiming for. This will make the rest of your plans fit into place.

 ### top tip for making a schedule

This is vital for any stag/hen night that has a theme or activities. You may have organised for a stripper or a practical joke to come at a certain time, or a mystery guest. It will be vital for all participants to be there (with camera equipment!) to enjoy the moment with you.

DO IT TOGETHER?

Elton and David certainly did – but will you? Deciding to spend the event separated or together will ultimately dictate the mood/theme of your stag or hen. Going it alone may well open the door to some X-rated fun, while spending the night together might mean you veer towards something more intimate and special.

Pros of going it alone

- It will prove that you can last more than 24 hours without each other.
- It is a sign of independence, both having equally strong friendship units.
- You'll have something to tell each other on your honeymoon.
- You can spend more time with your friends who you have known longer.

Cons of going it alone

- You may have mutual friends who would have to split up.
- It may feel unnecessary to segregate.
- There may be trust issues.
- There is the possibility of unbalanced levels of celebration – and hangover.

WHO'S IN CHARGE?

The first tradition with a stag or hen night is that it's mainly your friends or, in particular, a best friend who organises it for you. If you are planning on giving the responsibility to a friend, however, it might be worth lending this book to that person so they can look over the advice themselves. Unless you are in the position to trust this friend absolutely with the honour, you might find yourself fretting about their preparations, so it's worth setting a few guidelines before they begin. It's best to decide early on who will be the party leader, someone who knows the exact itinerary of your night, someone who has extra cash if there's any trouble and finally someone who can look after you when you're drunk.

COST SHARING

Alternatively, you and your partner may decide to split the cost of the celebrations between you to make things stretch that little further. Or one of you may consider paying for the whole thing, if perhaps the other partner has taken care of most of the reception and ceremony so far. Of course, you may have friends who state up front that they want to pay for everything.

WHOM TO INVITE

Depending on what your plans are, it is wise to have a rough idea of how many friends you will be inviting. You probably need a minimum of 10-12 and then onwards and upwards, depending on the scale of the evening. If it's a bar/club atmosphere, it will be easier to invite more guests than it will if you are doing an activity. Inevitably there will be the question of who gets on with whom, which can be tricky if it means not inviting certain people. Do your best not to let bitter rivals spoil your evening. An event like this could bring a distant group of friends back together.

Friends reunited

You might consider inviting friends from your school or college days, university, old home town, etc. It won't be everyday they'll get an invite to such a special event as an old friend's civil partnership, and if anyone does have any serious issues with 'gay marriage' then the chances are they'll turn the invitation down rather than turn up and start a rumpus.

The ex factor

Inviting exes to your stag do could put you into a Catch 22 situation. On the one hand it is an opportunity to show how amazingly better off you're doing since you last saw him/her, whilst on the other it brings the danger of upsetting your current partner. Either way, it is recommended not to overdose too heavily on ex-partners on your stag/hen do, as you'll probably be dealing with enough drama just with your close friends.

Your parents

This may seem completely ridiculous at first, but your civil partnership is a huge sign of responsibility, finally securing your place in the adult social mantle. Enjoying your 'last night of freedom' is a must, but you might want to let your parents see what they've been missing all these years. After they've witnessed most of what goes on, they'll be relieved that you've found someone and have decided to settle down!

 ## SET THE DATE

Tradition recommends that the stag or hen be held two weeks before the actual wedding (usually to allow the groom to get untied from the lamppost or get a tattoo removed). But if you are like most gay men and women and are no stranger to a night out on the town, a daring suggestion would be to have it on the very night before the big day. Years of clubbing experience will have surely increased your partying tolerance by now. Whatever you decide, try not to change it once you've agreed. Let everybody know in good time so they can plan any special surprises they might have for you.

 ## BUDGET

Everyone's financial position must be taken into account when planning your stag/hen do. It may be a case of asking your friends to blow as much as they can afford on a weekend of mass carnage. Take this into account when choosing from the different options for your stag/hen do and don't be afraid to ask your friends how much they will be willing to spend on a night out.

You could try and utilise a kitty policy for all purchases on your stag night. If you have decided on a party leader at this stage, then make them the treasurer. Having a kitty will have notable advantages:

• It prevents any tight-arses in your group from not getting their round in and will also alleviate the awkward situation of confronting them about it.

- People will stay with the group and are unlikely to break off into small cliques at different bars.
- All friends are then ensured to get absolutely blind drunk and enjoy it.

 ## TREAT YOUR FRIENDS

You love your friends and they love you – although they might not love you so much after they wake up £500 lighter and in need of a liver transplant. So before you go out with all your mates, demanding money to be poured into the drinks kitty, it might be worth realising exactly how much your guests will be forking out on the event as a whole. Maestro debit cards brought out a study claiming stag dos cost at least £30 more than hen dos, and further research has claimed that a national average of £300 per head is spent by guests on their married friends, so it's easy to see how things could go overboard. Although traditionally friends of the stag not only organise it but also chip in and divide the expenses between them, surprise all your chums and plan it yourself.

top tips for a great night

- **Discuss with each other.** Either discuss mutually with your partner or a best friend who you can rely on. Feel free to delegate the responsibility on to that friend.
- **Ask a friend.** Speak to those straight friends of yours who can offer pearls of wisdom when it comes to planning and organising.
- **Start your research.** Keep your eye out months in advance for all listings guides and favourite clubs that may have a special night on the date.
- **Decide on a budget.** Work out now who will pay what. Will there be any money behind the bar or do you expect your friends to foot the bill?
- **Make a date.** It's very important to the set the date in advance, so it can be convenient for all those invited.

PRANKS

Pranks are a tradition that many do not favour, though your friends could well be dying to stitch you up and may have already planned something for you. Why not play a prank on each other? Whether you are spending the night together or apart it will work either way. The main thing is to try arranging something both funny and original, you may want to tailor your own to your partner, here are some suggestions.

Trick him into thinking he's 'turned straight'

You or your friend's partner should be in charge of making this happen. It involves getting the man in question absolutely legless until he can't remember his own name. Get a female participant either a willing stranger or, better yet, a close friend to put him to bed. Whilst he's asleep she will leave condoms across the bed and kiss marks across his body. And when he finally comes to and asks what the hell happened the girl should give a convincing speech before capturing his reaction on camera. (Exchange gender for a female.)

Celebrity wedding

Musicians Whitney Houston and Bobby Brown spent their stag and hen nights together in their usual hell-raising form, racking up bar bills and trashing a hotel suite. They went against tradition, so why can't you?

Strippers

Yes, it's hardly original, but strippers dressed as police officers entering the stag venue usually raise a laugh, rather than accusations of sleaze.

Desertion

Leave the venue temporarily en mass when the guest of honour makes a trip to the toilet.

Personalised T-shirts

It's easy and cheap to print up T-shirts with a personal joke and accompanying image that you expose halfway through the celebrations. OK, you'll look like tourists in London, but this is all about good times, not glamour.

top tips for stag night novelties

- **Sex toys/condoms:** tacky but effectively embarrassing for all concerned.
- **Blow-up doll:** just to let everyone else know it's no ordinary stag night.
- **Old photos:** enlarged, with optional captions musing on fashion mistakes.
- **L-plates/wigs:** for unashamed comedic value.
- **Rubber sheep/chickens:** unacceptable for civil stags!

PUSH THE BOAT OUT

If you have the money under control and reason that you'll only be having the one stag night (we hope), why not push the boat out? Check out some ideas you may not have considered, such as going abroad or arranging an activities day.

Stag/hen weekends

Stag weekends have long been tradition and there's nothing to stop you jumping on the gay bandwagon and taking your friends away for a wild weekend. Where civil union stag weekends may differ is that cheap tarts and cocktails in Malaga might not be what you had in mind, so try something a little more cultural. Stag groups don't tend to choose cultural melting pots, favouring the cheaper Baltic states, such as Estonia and Latvia. This can work in the favour of the modern gay man; you are unlikely to get into bar room burping championships with rival groups and will also avoid disapproving stares from the locals.

top tips for weekends abroad

- **Berlin:** Gay nightlife, 24-hour bar licences, culture: Berlin has it all.
- **Amsterdam:** Red light district and delicious cakes.
- **New York:** Shopping, culture and famous hot spots.
- **France:** Wine, food, and gorgeous Frenchmen.

FIVE WAYS TO SPEND YOUR STAG NIGHT

If you want to do something more structured than just roaming from club to club, the following suggestions might give you some ideas.

Stag night: the rivals

One for those couples who really do share mutual friends: it's war. This consists of painstakingly separating your friends into two groups, preferably of equal numbers. You then disperse into teams, e.g. Team Ben vs Team Jamie, who have to compete with each other to have the most outrageous stag night in history. Photographic evidence will play a big part here, as will video phone equipment and rendezvous meeting points to check up on all activities throughout the night.

Organise it for your other half

The simple way to deal with two stag nights, if you've decided to spend them apart, is to organise them for one another. That way you can be in complete control of what your partner gets up too, a great option for all control freaks. If you and your partner are of different ages you may have different ideas of having a good time, but you'll know each other well enough by now to know what the other one likes best. If you are particularly brave, you will agree to keep all celebratory plans as a surprise.

Party and pamper

Partying and pampering on a stag weekend is usually the preferred option for brides-to-be, but this shouldn't put off those who aren't afraid to look after themselves. Book for either yourself and your partner or a few friends to have a day in a luxury spa. Treat yourself to a full body massage, steam rooms, facials and even a good old waxing. This will either serve to get you ready for a night out on the town or a sensible calm and cleanse before the big day.

Celebrity stag

If you want a night like Elton and David's, well think again. Unless you are friends with the former president of America and most of the world's A-List you'll have a tough act to follow. However, it won't be hard to create your own version of the celebrity stag do. Considering Elton held his at the London club Too2Much (available for hire) it shouldn't be impossible to tempt a few C-listers and some press attention, depending on how extravagant your plans are. Remember to keep the guests happy with champagne and canapés.

Make it a quiet night one

This is ideal for those of you who are past your wild clubbing days and favour romantic evenings in together. Really break tradition and wait to see your friends and family at the party. Sit back and take stock of how far you've come and what a wonderful future you have in store. Stay in and cook with a classic DVD and a bottle of fine wine, have a candle-lit dinner for two or book a night in a luxury hotel. Whatever you do, make it just the two of you.

top tips for a traditional night

If you want to try your hand at irony during your stag celebrations, why not choose from some of the classic heterosexual stag night options and have a boys' night out at one of the following?

- **Night at the dogs:** Get your mates down to the dog track for an evening of thrills, spills, frantic gesticulating and triumphant singing.
- **Go to a strip club:** A little harder to find than Stringfellows and possibly more seedy, check listings for strip nights in local gay pubs and clubs.
- **Trip on the Party Bus:** '70s/'80s theme nights, nightclubbing and bar crawling. If it's tasteless, it'll be on the apparently world-famous Party Bus!

BE PROUD – BE SAFE

The very last thing you want on your stag night is trouble. Depending on how you feel this may already dictate where you'd want to spend your stag party. We've come a long way, and now with civil partnerships we're feeling increasingly on level footing with everyone else. Just be aware if you are not in a gay environment there will always be people ready to ruin the moment. There's no shame in celebrating what should be the happiest day of your lives, so be proud; but be wary that we still live in a society where some people don't like to see happiness in people different from them.

We're not suggesting you will be the victim of a homophobic attack, but things can get out of hand when alcohol and emotions are running high. Look out for the following potential flashpoints and ensure they don't join you on the night!

- **An ex in attendance.** So he or she still doesn't see that you're the happiest person alive. Don't let that put you off. After all, you're getting married in the morning!

- **A bitter friend.** He (or she) might try to ruin your night but rise above it. He probably feels he has your best interests at heart.
- **The bouncer.** Slow down, try and remember not everyone knows it is your stag do, shut up and let your slightly more sober friends do all the talking.

CAN YOU KEEP A SECRET?

This will only apply to those having separate stag nights we hope, but one time-honoured tradition is that whatever happens on the stag night, stays there! Any leaking of sensitive information is an absolute no-no, so make the silence is golden rule is clear to all your friends. Then all you have to do is remember to enjoy what will surely be one of the wildest nights of your (by now) professional partying careers!

VOX-POP

Barry, 60, and Andre, 39, Huddersfield

'Living in a town like Huddersfield with a small gay community, we decided to have the stag party in the only gay club, although one of us is knocking on 60! We were holding the ceremony at Cedar Court, and the club is just around the corner, so if things had got really out of hand we wouldn't have had to go far the next day!

'We started off the celebrations at a restaurant then, after getting suitably drunk there, we went on to Chads, the only gay club in the village! We say, have a right knees-up for your stag night, because you'll only have the one – hopefully! You're bound to have a lot of relatives at the wedding party, like we did, so your stag night is the time you can really let loose without having to apologise for it.'

chapter 8

The Guests

With the advent of civil partnerships, members of the gay community can now openly and publicly declare their love for one another in an 'official' way. For some individuals, this will involve coming out of the closet, if they had not been able to already. Therefore, it is important to consider the guest list carefully, making sure that news of the ceremony is well received among all the invited prospective guests. Invitations themselves require thought and deliberation, especially when it comes to friends and family. You must ensure you tell any friends and family members of your plans, if they are likely to hear about the event through mutual friends. Alternatively, you may choose to keep the ceremony fairly private and low key, so a substantial guest list will be unnecessary.

Having decided on the civil ceremony and reception, it's time to pinpoint guest list details and keep numbers down according to budget and capacity restraints, particularly if you are having an engagement party, too. Getting together an address and contact notebook might be a handy place to start.

 ## DID YOU KNOW?

In a traditional heterosexual wedding, the custom of the bride and groom surrounding themselves with a wedding party of close friends originated from an era when the bride was captured from her family. The groom gathered a group of supporters with him to divert the bride's family while he whisked her away. Once the bride had been triumphantly captured, he sent his closest associate otherwise known as his best man to quell her family's tempers. At the same time, the bride relied on close friends to console and ease her concerns in her new social set-up.

PREPARING THE GUEST LIST

Preparing a guest list isn't a simple task. Firstly you will usually have to compromise with your partner about just how many people can attend from both social groups. The size of your families is also a consideration. Additionally, you must usually allow for a 'plus one' where friends' partners will be included. Often, both sets of parents, if invited, will want all family members in attendance, and this may present a logistical nightmare, depending on how large your family is. Friends may take precedence over family, and in this instance a great deal of tact and diplomacy must be exercised to avoid insult and resentment. If young children are not invited, their parents may have to find babysitters, which could be problematic. Although there may be people who will be upset at your decisions, be firm yet thoughtful to reduce stress levels and prevent any nasty arguments.

In the past, convention has dictated that the bride's mother compiles the guest list in consultation with the groom's parents. However, when it comes to a civil partnership, the person(s) footing the reception bill may be a more appropriate choice. As a general rule, 80 per cent of those invited will attend, so use that as a rough guide. Additionally, last-minute cancellations may allow you to invite anyone you were unable to include first time around. Make sure you send out any late invitations less than three weeks before the civil partnership, to avoid any embarrassing situations.

DRAFT LIST

A draft guest list will help you to calculate approximate numbers and can concurrently be used for recording gifts from guests and those who are unable to attend the civil partnership. Have a rubber and pencil at the ready, or make sure you back up any Excel documents, as the first list may not be watertight. It's a good idea to divide any drafts into three categories: definite, probable and possible. You may recall close friends and relations before considering work colleagues and acquaintances so double check before starting to compile the master list. Useful points of contact may include mobile phone and e-mail address books, and extra family contacts gleaned from your parents' Christmas card list! Relatives in the couple's immediate family are usually included. Again, the same follows with aunts, uncles, cousins and stepfamily members. As a rule of thumb, try to make the guest list split 50/50 from both bride's and groom's sides to be as fair as possible.

Of course, this will depend on the size of the families and whether good relations are maintained between your prospective spouse and his or her kin.

If the guest list is too long and you have over-exceeded the budget and any reception capacity restraints, you will need to cut it down. This will often be a selective process that may provoke a lively debate between parties. To help matters, you have the option of inviting friends to the evening celebration only, depending on how many parties you intend to have. If the ceremony venue is very limiting (which it may well be in many civil registry arenas), guests may be invited to the reception only. The registrar may also be invited with his or her spouse, if you wish.

In the case of a large civil partnership, where there will be in excess of 100 or more guests, a number of questions should be posed:

- Can any of those invited bring guests? If so, how many additional people can be brought?
- If there are 20 cousins but the couple are only close to a few of them, how many should be invited?
- Will children be invited? This needs to be made clear on the invitation to avoid any sticky situations. Some people may opt for an adults-only civil partnership depending on the theme or the nature of late-night celebrations.

FINAL LIST

When the draft list has been devised (with both sets of parents, if appropriate) and the timetable and budget checklists have been drawn up, it can be finalised with specific detail for those with any special dietary requirements. A percentage of guests might also be either vegetarians or vegans, so make sure you get it right! Exceptional consideration must also be given when it comes to ordering high chairs for young children and any necessary provisions for disabled guests. The final list must also include anyone who cannot be invited, but for whom a letter informing them of the civil partnership is deemed essential.

The final list will also help you to draft and send thank-you letters without having to compile an additional chart, in effect killing two birds with one stone. Acceptances and refusals should be tallied accordingly. It may be an idea to invite gift donors to dinner at some point after the civil partnership.

INVITATIONS CHECKLIST

Repeat this mini-checklist for everyone on your guest list:

Name	
Address	
Telephone	
E-mail	
Ceremony	
Reception	
Evening	
Invitation sent	
Accepted/refused	
Special needs	
Gift received	
Thank-you note sent	
Cake sent	

TRAVELLING GUESTS

Hopping on a plane from Sydney to London to attend your big day? If any close relatives or friends are travelling some serious mileage to wish you happiness, make sure they feel appreciated! Prepare for their arrival thoroughly, and finalise any accommodation reservations, if necessary. It is also important to include them in any thank-you speeches, as a sign of courtesy. Your or your partner's parents' may offer them the option of staying at their house. However, some guests may prefer to stay in a hotel or guesthouse, so ensure they have detailed information of the locality. Provide them with maps, telephone numbers and any pre-ceremony festivities if relevant.

STATIONERY

Your stationery gives you the opportunity to reach out to your guest and provide them with a first impression of your civil partnership. There may be speculation about the occasion, as it's relatively new, so make your invitations clear and concise to dispel any myths or queries about your union. Choose a design that will reflect the tone and ambience of the day.

Pre-civil partnership stationery

Before you send out your civil partnership invitations, you might like to consider further stationery options. This could include invitations to your stag or hen nights; or rehearsal invitations, should you and your partner fancy a run-through to cast away any last-minute jitters.

Save-the-date cards

Save-the-date cards are a fabulous way of announcing the date of your civil partnership well in advance to make sure there are no untimely double bookings. This is particularly useful if the event is taking place in the summer, when people might be jetting off to foreign climes. These nifty cards are also useful for overseas guests who will need to plan their trip.

These cards are generally sent out around three to six months before a civil partnership, although you could send them out up to a year before, depending on how organised you are. Ideally, they should be compact and match the invitations that will follow. Send them out either in an envelope or online, whichever is easier for you. Depending on who is hosting the wedding, they should be sent either by the couple, or by the parents.

Bear in mind that you may not feel the need to send one to every guest, and that everyone who receives a card must be on your final guest list. Once you've asked them to keep the date free, you can't cross them off the list!

Rehearsal dinner invitations

Following on from conventional wedding traditions, a civil partnership rehearsal can be held a few days or the day before the wedding. It is an opportunity to run through the words and moves of the day ahead of time.

Heterosexual etiquette dictates that the groom's parents host a rehearsal dinner, which is held the night before the wedding, given as a courtesy to the bride's parents, who host the wedding. Of course in the case of a civil partnership, it is up to both sets of parents (if invited) to decide who will host the dinner. Invitations to the rehearsal dinner are usually formal, but should be used as a guide to how you, your partner or the relevant 'in-laws' would like to be addressed.

While the rehearsal dinner should not compete with the civil partnership, it is usual for the invitations to complement the civil partnership invitations, but not match them. Invitations should be sent out around two weeks before the occasion.

SELECTING YOUR CIVIL PARTNERSHIP INVITATIONS

As a rule of thumb, invitations to heterosexual civil weddings have been designed with a modern twist. However, you can change the blueprint and come up with a design you feel comfortable with. A classic invitation is simply typed (no graphics), ideally engraved on good-quality white or cream card. The format is an upright, folded card with the wording on one side only. Black or silver lettering is the most popular. If you have chosen a traditional, specially printed or engraved card, the guest's name is handwritten at the top left-hand side.

For themed weddings, you might choose to have invitations that complement the theme. For example, a Robin Hood themed wedding might come phrased with medieval English vernacular on a parchment or scroll-effect card.

WHERE TO SHOP AND WHAT TO BUY

Your stationery can be purchased from a number of sources. These include mail order, printer, stationers and stationery designers, or you can buy online. You might even decide to create your own stationery. Just be careful that your design does not clutter the basic details and contact information.

The variety of items and styles is often huge, so have a vague idea before you dive in. You might expect simply to choose the invitation style you want, and then have it printed and supplied with matching envelopes. Certainly in some instances this may be the case, but there are many other stationery items available that you might like to consider:

- Envelope seals
- Response cards
- Place cards
- Napkins and napkin rings
- Coasters
- Guest scrolls
- Menus
- Adhesive bottle labels
- Seed sticks
- Personalised ribbon

- After dinner mints with personalised wrappers (yum!)
- Guest autograph album
- Cake boxes
- Thank-you cards

This list looks extensive, but don't get carried away. If you decide to have everything on offer, your civil partnership will be saturated with stationery. Also, as cute as some of these items are, it's not wise to splash out too heavily if you're working to a tight financial plan. However, it should also be said that many of these items offer charming keepsakes and at least some are worth considering. They can also provide a wonderful way of continuing a theme for your wedding.

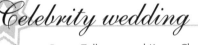

Celebrity wedding

Actress Renee Zellweger and Kenny Chesney kept their ceremony a secret by marrying in the US Virgin Islands. No need for a large guest list, then!

WELL-BEHAVED GUESTS

It's not all about the couple, you know; guests have a crucial role to play in proceedings, too. If you feel that any of your guests need reminding, you could leave this book lying around open at this page, or just make a few suggestions on how you expect them to behave to make sure everything goes without a hitch.

- Being late is not a fashion statement! If the ceremony begins at four, guests should arrive fifteen minutes early to give themselves time to find a seat and get settled.
- It is distracting – and frankly fairly rude! – to take photographs during the ceremony as it is the crucial part of the proceedings and may put the happy couple off. Leave the ceremony photography to the professionals, and save your snaps for later.
- Guests who are unable to attend the ceremony may still be gracious and send a gift. Do make sure you write to thank them.
- Guests should not expect to be able to bring a date unless you have specifically invited them. The cost for each person attending a wedding is generally very high, so bringing unexpected guests is discourteous.

- Hopefully your guests will RSVP promptly so you can make the necessary decisions on numbers. Additionally, if they have to cancel after they've accepted, you should expect them to do so as soon as possible. If you have not had a reply from any of your guests, perhaps a polite reminder – along the lines of 'we are looking forward to seeing you at the wedding' – would prompt them into action.
- While the reception is a time for everyone to enjoy themelves and congratulate the happy couple, it is possible that some might get too drunk and embarrass themselves! Perhaps a word in their ear wouldn't go amiss that you hope they know their limits. If all else fails, designate someone to look after them so you don't have to do it yourselves.

PERSONALISED STATIONERY

Personalised stationery is becoming very trendy and for those big on image, it's a must-have luxury. For completely bespoke stationery, you could commission a stationery designer. This is one way of putting a personal touch to your plans, but bear in mind it will almost certainly take longer to deliver than pre-printed items. A first consultation with the designer should really take place around four or five months before the civil partnership.

Prices will naturally be higher than for mass-produced stationery, but by how much will depend on the amount of work involved, the quality of the paper used and the number of items ordered. It is vital to fix a deadline for completion and the price at the beginning, in order to avoid any unwarranted surprises.

Invitations

Invitations are accessible in virtually any design you choose and specialist companies can even offer you the option of having your invitation personalised by having a picture of your registry office/reception venue printed on them. Don't forget that you will need separate invitations for those being invited to the evening reception only and there is also the choice of including response cards together with printed envelopes.

Reception stationery

Once you've chosen the theme of your wedding stationery, you can continue the same design throughout your reception, with tableware that will match the style of your invitations and can add a sense of erudition to your celebrations.

Place cards

Place cards are crucial if you have a seating plan, so that guests know where to sit. Names can be printed by printer or stationery designer or you might write them by hand.

Menu cards

Menu cards can be printed for the guests and placed on each table. However, you shouldn't feel under any kind of obligation to provide them and this should be considered within the remit of your budget. Your hotel or reception venue may be able to supply these for you at a lower price, so do your homework.

Favour boxes

The tradition of giving bonbonnières to celebrate a special occasion dates back to early European history. They were given to celebrate marriages, birthdays and christenings by the wealthy aristocrats of the period. Each favour box (or even bag) traditionally contains sugared almonds symbolising health, wealth, happiness, fertility and long life. Often used as place settings, they make a wonderful way of saying thank you to your guests.

 top tip for distributing cake

Small boxes with greaseproof inner linings can be used to send out portions of wedding cake to absent friends, personalised to match your overall theme. You can also include compliment cards. Bags can be provided for those guests at the reception who want to nosh on their slice of cake at home.

 ADDITIONAL ITEMS

If all that isn't enough, why not push out the ornate boat with monogrammed napkins, napkin rings, drink mats, matchbooks and thank-you cards? For a more unique, unusual touch why not try pre-printed ribbon, balloons and bottle labels. However, while all of these items may seem very attractive they can be an extravagant luxury and are certainly not essential items.

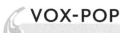

VOX-POP

How many guests do you want at your civil partnership?

Saffron Chaise, 26, dramatist

'The more the merrier. I'm larger than life so I want a larger than life ceremony, please!'

Elizabeth Wilber, 29, corporate banker

'I want lots of people at my civil partnership, all my friends, family and people who have meant a lot to me throughout the years.'

chapter 9

What To Wear

There has been lots of debate and speculation about what couples should wear on the day of their civil partnership. In line with traditional etiquette, the man (men) should wear a suit of some description, while the woman (women) should wear a wedding dress. However, many gay and lesbian partnerships may not feel comfortable and familiar with these rigid stereotypical ideas. Some gay men may identify with softer, more feminine outfits, while some lesbians may feel more at ease in boyish, loose-fitting garments. For this purpose, we have divided this chapter into several sections incorporating conventional and alternative clothing. This will help to encompass a good diversity of designs to enable each individual to feel relaxed and secure during his/her civil partnership.

TRADITIONAL STYLE

For him (or for her, if she would prefer to wear men's clothes)

Heterosexual weddings always have the groom in a smart, stylish suit, and if you want to play safe, there is no reason why a civil partnership can't follow the same guidelines. You can still express your individuality in the colour of your tie and matching accessories.

What's the story, morning glory?

Traditionally speaking, the men in a wedding party don smart, formal attire to complement the bride. A morning suit, together with a silk top hat, gloves and a waistcoat, is customary for an official occasion. A conventional morning suit is a black or grey tailcoat with pinstripe trousers, white collar and a grey tie. As a general rule, dark colours are worn for winter and afternoon civil partnerships. Don't wear a light coloured suit in winter; it's more likely to get dirty on your way to and from the ceremony. However, morning suits are available in a range of colours, so get creative if black and grey aren't your favourite shades.

Accessories such as the waistcoat, cummerbund (waist sash), tie, handkerchief and buttonhole, can be co-ordinated with the attire of your partner and any other male members of the party. In a wedding ceremony, the hat is removed upon entering a church, so you might want to consider removing your hat while the ceremony is taking place. You can also remove your gloves while vows are being exchanged. Pragmatically speaking, the hat and gloves tend to be worn for the photographs, as they are an essential part of the morning dress and really accentuate a chic and well-turned-out ensemble.

The shirt usually worn with a morning suit is typically white, with a plain collar and dress tie or a high-winged collar worn with a cravat. You could also consider a bow tie or an ascot. The tie can be coloured, perhaps to match your partner's colour scheme. If you and your partner are concerned about matching fabrics or styles, take a sample from the shop to compare. You'll also need to choose from single-breasted and double-breasted jackets and collars that are peaked, notched or shawl.

Shoes and socks are generally black. The groom's shoes should have little to no embellishment, and are generally patent leather. It is also traditional to wear cufflinks, a tie tack, and a boutonnière that matches any flowers or bouquets.

Many people opt for hiring morning suits, rather than buying. Be sure to choose a reputable firm and book well in advance. The groom(s) and any other male members of the party should be measured for their suits approximately three months before the wedding.

Any attendants who live further away should go to a local shop for measurements, and then send the information to the groom so that he can set up the rental. Make sure that your attendants understand that they are not to make their own hire arrangements elsewhere. These members of the wedding party should try to arrive at least two to three days before the civil partnership for final measurements, in case of last minute alterations.

Most suits can be picked up a day or two in advance. It is crucial to check clothes carefully before leaving the shop. Look for any stains, rips, or possible cigarette burns. Everyone should try on their suit to be sure it fits properly and to ensure the length of the trousers and jacket sleeves are correct. Be sure to wear the shoes you will be wearing at the civil partnership for this. Check the cuffs and collar for frayed material, and search for any missing buttons on jackets.

After the civil partnership, the best man usually returns his and the grooms' suits to the formalwear shop by the next working day.

Attendants are responsible for returning their own suits, also by the next trading day to avoid late charges. Minor food or beverage stains can be removed easily enough; if a suit is heavily damaged, though, be prepared to pay for it. So chaps, be careful during the big day: no unwanted spillages in any conspicuous areas!

top tip for sartorial elegance

Make sure you have a handkerchief. It's always a classy touch!

Lounge suits

Positively less formal, lounge suits do exactly what they say on the tin! They are a very popular choice and may be worn again after the civil partnership. Again, the shirt should be white and the tie should be pale blue or grey with relatively little patterning. Many heterosexual grooms' wear lounge suits to a wedding held in a registry office. A lounge suit is also deemed to be appropriate for a widow(er) or those having a wedding or civil partnership for the second time.

Celebrity wedding

Fancy something flamboyant? Cameraman Daniel Moder chose to wed movie star A-lister Julia Roberts wearing a red ruffled shirt and tan-coloured slacks. Now that's creative! Julia's wedding dress consisted of a pale pink cotton halter dress with hand-painted flowers, and embroidered pearls and antique beads.

For her (or for him if he would prefer to wear women's clothes)

When it comes to wedding dresses, each one has to be as individual and unique as the bride wearing it. No two pieces are exactly the same and there is not a single style that will suit everyone. Aside from the initial dress shape, you must also consider which necklines to go for, which accessories and veils to choose, and that's just the start of it! Here are a few ideas for a little inspiration.

FASHION TERMS EXPLAINED

- A-line skirt: close-fitting waist, flared hemline
- Ballerina skirt: full skirt that falls to the ankles
- Bell sleeve: long sleeve that flares from top arm to waist
- Bolero: jacket to waist, without collar, mostly worn open
- Bouffant: puffed, baggy
- Bustle: pad or frame puffing out top of skirt behind
- Dropped waist: long waist that falls below actual waistline
- Fitted bodice: tight-fitting top
- Juliet cap: fitted cap worn at back of head

Fabric

- Batiste: thin and fine, such as cotton or rayon
- Brocade: woven with raised design
- Chintz: cotton, generally glazed
- Crepe: thin crinkled cotton or rayon
- Organza: sheer silk or synthetic fabric
- Raw Silk: natural silk
- Satin: smooth glossy, such as silk, rayon or nylon
- Tulle: fine netting

Ball gown

Strapless is great if you are tall, slim and broad shouldered. If you have the height, but are narrow around your shoulders or feel over-exposed in such a revealing cut, go for a more covered-up version with sleeves, straps or a high neck. This style can still work if you are of medium height or veer towards pear-shape in build, as you can emphasise your waist and conceal wider hips with a fuller skirt. This corseted style can also work with a curvaceous bust by leading the eye towards the waist. Higher shoes and hair tied up can accentuate a slender silhouette. Our top tip is to wear long operatic gloves, which look fabulous with a strapless gown, elongating arm length and creating a demure demeanour. If you are planning on having a train, then the ball gown is best suited to this. Consider whether you want the train to be attached or detached, and how long or short you would like it to be.
Recommended designer examples: Simply Brides, Christine Frances
Celebrity examples: Christine Baumgartner, Britney Spears

Princess line

With gorgeous lines and a flattering bodice, this style is perfect for creating an impression that is uncluttered, and emphatic in its large expanse of uninterrupted fabric. This is such a versatile, adaptable style that it can be tailor-made to suit most builds and heights. It is particularly effective on tall curvy figures, and is great at creating an illusion of rounder, fuller curves on even the most flat-chested of individual! It is essential to get the right underwear to disguise broader hips and bums, while concurrently pulling in the waistline. Shorter, less busy styles are great for more petite, boyish frames. If you have a long body and relatively diminutive legs, the high waistline and swell of the skirt can help proportion you. There are a variety of neckline options that work well for the princess line. If the cut falls straight down from the shoulder seam, the dress works well with a high neck, while the curved line draws across the breast from the armhole and benefits rounder, bateau (boat) and scoop necks. The bateau neckline is one that closely follows the collarbone. It is a good choice for women who have well-proportioned necks and heads, but who wish to present a more conservative appearance. The neckline softly follows the curve of the collarbone, high in both the front and back, opening wide at the sides and ending in shoulder seams.

Recommended designer examples: Orchid Brides
Celebrity examples: Queen Sofia of Spain, Letizia Ortiz Rocasolano

Empire line

The style is universally accepted as well-suited for most physiques. The high waistline lengthens the body and hides any unsightly lumps or bumps. It is superlative for those with a smaller bust or a long, lithe build. It also flatters those with an hour-glass figure. The Empire line can also help to minimise larger breasts if it worn correctly and also is the top choice for any pregnant brides. Add a touch of glamour with sparkling straps or classic, elegant folds along the fabric.

Recommended designer examples: Romantica of Devon
Celebrity examples: Kate Winslett, Liv Tyler, Emily Mortimer

Mermaid and fishtail

Bias-cut wedding dresses tend to be simple, graceful and dramatic. They were inspired from the 1930s bias-cut evening gowns. You don't necessarily need to be very tall to carry off this style, but being slim and athletic is a definite advantage. Be warned that underwear is also advised against, as the cut tends to cling to every bodily contour so make sure you feel comfortable going commando. If you are very skinny or flat chested you may be better off opting for a slip dress or a more constructed design, as the volume of the dress can balance hips and bust more effectively. The style also looks great with ornate cowls draped over the back of the garment. This is also a fitting dress to wear if you have chosen a beach-themed or seaside wedding, although plunging into the ocean fully-clothed may not be advisable!

Recommended designer examples: Ian Stuart, Hannah Woodhouse
Celebrity examples: Holly Hunter

A-line

A very popular and widely seen style, this dress can be very flattering and alluring, as long as you get your proportions correct. Like the Empire line, this dress can extend and stretch a more petite frame, and the waist can emphasise a voluptuous figure. The dress masks a pear-shaped body, while halter necks, deep plunging scoops or picture collars make for a spectacular impression. Got a great set of pins? Then raise that hemline as far as a mini-dress for something a little more daring and revealing. Optionally, go for the more conservative train effect for something more conventional. Be sure to check that your shoes are comfortable or you'll end up with blisters galore.

Recommended designer examples: Valentino, Dior
Celebrity examples: Jennifer Lopez

Column

Symmetry may not be the order of the day, so why not go for an asymmetrical neckline? This can help to add height to those requiring elevation, or those with sexy shoulders looking to show them off. However, this style will not suit those who require a bra for support. Dress lengths can be individually customised. Typically, cavernous inverted pleats at the back of the garment help to maintain a slim silhouette, while allowing for movement and volume accentuated by the bustled contours of the dress. This design is not well-suited to those with a pear-shaped figure, or those with a tall and skinny physique. Add a bold collar to draw attention to the collarbone and detract from a smaller bust.

Recommended designer examples: Amanda Wyatt
Celebrity examples: Jennifer Aniston

Mini and midi

This more unusual style is only suited to those with a thinner, more athletic physique, although the knee-length shift styles can be more alluring for those with a more rounded bust. This style is far more modern and daring in appearance, so probably best avoided at a conservative ceremony. To reveal more at the reception, some detachable panels will transform a full-length dress to a mini, which will allow more freedom and an accessible fit.

Recommended designer examples: White Mischief, Organza
Celebrity examples: Christine Aguilera

Wedding suits

Recent civil partnerships that took place before this book was published have shown that many lesbian couples chose to wear matching suits on their special day. Although, it is difficult to predict whether this trend will continue, we anticipate that some women will feel more relaxed in a suit, whether it is made-to-fit for a man or woman. There are many suits that will flatter your figure. As with a dress, a suit can disguise or accentuate any problem areas of your body. Short, waist-length jackets can proportion elfin, diminutive physiques, whereas long line jackets or a 1940s-inspired peplum style with a nipped waist can help shape a flat silhouette. A draped peplum also gives an unusual look to the hipline, similar to a vintage design. If you are more voluptuous, try a shorter jacket that will direct the eye to your waist. Full, expansive skirts and Edwardian flared equestrian jackets will accentuate the hour-glass figure. If you fancy a more conservative suit, specialist tailors will customise blazers in a range of cashmeres, silks and linens, as well as suede if you fancy something really different. Sartorial shopping has never been so refreshing!

Recommended designer examples: Hugo Boss, Ann Taylor Loft, Ghost
Celebrity examples: None as yet. Go on: set the trend!

 top tip for imaginative ideas

As wedding fashions continue to evolve separately from the general vogue, people now feel freer to allow their imaginations a full rein and some wedding parties are not so much in best dress as fancy dress. See Chapter 4 Just For You (pages 41–6) for details on how to theme your civil partnership for a truly unique occasion!

DID YOU KNOW?

Married in:

- White: You've chosen all right
- Blue: Your love is true
- Pearl: You'll live in a whirl
- Brown: You'll live out of town
- Red: You'll wish yourself dead
- Yellow: You're ashamed of your fellow
- Green: Ashamed to be seen
- Pink: Your fortunes/spirits will sink
- Grey: You'll live far away
- Black: You'll wish yourself back

NB: It is considered bad luck to wear green, unless the bride is Irish.

Accessories

Once you've settled on a dress design, it's time to think about the accessories, which can make or break an outfit.

Trains are extensions of the fabric at the back of the skirt and are mostly suited to formal dress at upmarket events. More traditional trains trail yards behind the bride and are often weighty and fairly heavy. Shorter trains can be more convenient to wear and equally attractive.

Tiaras and other ornate headpieces can complement a formal dress with a full veil. Tiaras, comb clips, Alice bands or circlets can be used to secure certain types of veil. Tiaras with real or paste gems were popular with more conventional white dresses in weddings, and are a real asset to accentuate a feminine dress.

Often seen as the most symbolic outward piece of attire, the veil was originally designed to cover a bride's face during the wedding ceremony. Although many lesbian couples may not decide to wear a veil due to quintessentially heterosexual conventions, the veil can be a great aesthetically pleasing piece if worn with the right dress. As a rule of thumb, the smarter the dress, the longer the veil but obviously the length and density of the veil will vary.

Shoes should be bought, dyed or covered to match the dress in colour and fabric. Raw silk or synthetic materials are fairly commonplace and radiant elegance against a well-suited outfit. The bride(s) should bear in mind that the shoes will be worn for a long day, so comfort must be a priority. Don't go over the top with heel height and check that your soles aren't slippery; if they are, scratch them to get a rough, scored surface. Practise walking to avoid any embarrassing trips on the day. For budget spenders, buy a pair of shoes that can be worn again or try off-season shoes for a thrifty purchase.

As with other accessories, lingerie should be purchased after the dress has been chosen. Be careful when choosing the colour of your underwear to prevent any dark shadows creeping through your gown. White and pastel colour shades remain a popular choice. Try on any matching bra and knickers sets first to ensure a snug but comfortable fit.

Wearing simple yet visually striking jewellery will keep the dress the focal point of any onlookers' gaze. Wearing something on your neckline jewellery shows off an exposed collarbone. Generally a bride(s) does not wear a watch as time is not a consideration for her. Try on all your jewellery and other accessories to make sure everything sits well together. If you have an engagement ring, transfer it to your right hand early in the day: one less thing to remember at the ceremony. But if your engagement ring locks into the civil partnership band, your partner will need this in advance to pass to the chief attendant.

ALTERNATIVE STYLE

Men wear suits and women wear bridal gowns. Period. However, if this traditional protocol doesn't really cut it for, why not defy convention and reach out to pastures new and truly personalise your own civil partnership ceremony? If you and your partner are involved in a particular scene such as the S&M community, then maybe PVC will be preferable to polyester, or a corset preferable to a corsage?

You might be lucky enough to have local outlets for outrageous and unusual attire. If not, the internet is a fabulous resource for just about everything you could possibly desire, from fantasy to Gothic or sci-fi. See page 151 for some website suggestions.

VOX-POP
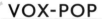

What do you and your partner plan to wear at your civil partnership?

Anna Jackson, 25, HR

'Definitely a dress! It's going to be my wedding day so I want it to be something traditional!'

Liz Underhill, 27, investment banker

'I'd also want to wear a dress like Anna. We're both pretty femme I guess, so I'd want my attire to reflect that.'

chapter 10

The Ceremony

So, what actually takes place during the ceremony of a civil partnership? What needs to be said? Is it complicated?

Well, actually, no. The ceremony itself is very similar to a civil wedding and takes on average between 12 to 16 minutes. However, it needn't be rushed and usually municipal registrars offer couples a variety of vows to make sure the couple gets the most from the ceremony. What follows is a basic guide to how a civil partnership ceremony works, although it is important to remember that vows can be personalised and modified (excluding the statutory legal vernacular).

On arrival at the approved premises, the Superintendent Registrar will meet the couple privately to explain the procedure. Meanwhile, the guests will gather together in the designated marriage room. The Superintendent Registrar and the couple then enter the room and the ceremony takes place.

The registrar will welcome guests and the couple saying: 'Today they will affirm their love and publicly declare their commitment to each other.' The registrar will then ask if anyone knows any reason why the couple cannot form a civil partnership. (Your partner might not find it amusing if your best friend raises his hand, for a joke!) The following words will then be read out. '(Your name) and (your partner's name) have chosen to pledge themselves to each other by committing to a legally binding contract. Their partnership will enable the love and respect that they have for each other to develop into a deep and lasting relationship. We, who are witnessing your civil partnership, hope that despite the stresses inevitable in any life, your love, trust and understanding of each other, will increase your contentment and heighten your joy in living.'

The couple can choose between the following vows:

'I (your name) pledge to share my life openly with (your partner's name). I promise to cherish and tenderly care for you, to honour and encourage you. I

will respect you as an individual and be true to you through good times and bad. To these things I give my word.'

Or,

'I (your name) choose you above all others, to share my life. I promise to honour this pledge as long as I live.'

The couple will then exchange rings, stating:

'This ring is a token of my abiding love and a sign of the promise I make to you today.'

The registrar can then say the following words, which are optional.

'Every day you live, you learn how to receive love with as much understanding as you give it. Find things within yourself, then you can share them with each other. Do not fear this love. Have an open heart and a sincere mind. Be concerned with each other's happiness. Be constant and consistent in your love. From this will come security and strength.'

There will then be the signing of the civil partnership schedule and the presentation of a commemorative certificate.

The final sign off will be:

'Now that the ceremony is over and the experience of living day by day as legal partners is about to begin, go and meet it gladly.'

After the ceremony has taken place, the Superintendent Registrar leaves the premises.

REAL LIFE

Of course, the size and length of the ceremony will vary greatly depending on the number of guests and the couple's choice to say any additional words. Matt and I attended a civil partnership at Islington Town Hall, based in North London, with around 30 guests invited to witness the union of Efstathia Balta, 29, and Michelle Lea Hunt, 25. The happy couple came into the main chamber room together, accompanied by the music of Tori Amos. Of course, music is entirely optional, but many couples choose to have a memorable song or soundtrack to add ambience and atmosphere to the occasion. The group of attendants included a photographer and two witnesses, as is customary at a civil wedding. The couple were asked a number of set questions by the registrar (similar to those above) and then signed the civil register after they had exchanged rings. This is an important symbolic act, and I foresee many couples opting to give rings to one another as an outward declaration of their love.

THE RING

The wedding ring has always represented the concrete sealing of the marriage pact. A civil partnership ring bears much the same meaning, and many couples have exchanged rings in many of the civil partnerships that have taken place in this country today. Of course, there is a big market for such a precious commodity, and many gay-owned or gay-friendly companies now stock a fantastic, versatile collection of rings (see page 152). From classic wedding ring bands to diamond-set wedding bands, there is something for everyone. From stainless steel to silver, engraved to emerald, you are sure to find something beautiful and ornate if you scratch the surface a little.

DID YOU KNOW?

In ancient cultures it was believed that the third finger of the left hand, had a special vein called vena amoris, the vein of love. This ran from the ring finger directly to the heart. There is, of course, no scientific basis for this romantic theory, but the custom has endured throughout generations. It was King Edward VI of England who decreed that the third finger of the left hand be designated as the official ring finger. In 1549, the *Book of Common Prayer* sealed the deal with the designation of the left hand as the marriage hand.

Celebrity wedding

For Brad Pitt, buying a ready-made diamond for Jennifer Aniston wasn't good enough! He had one made to his instructions and also designed their wedding bands. The Aside band in white gold with 18 carat diamonds was the result. What a considerate chap!

PERSONALISING YOUR CIVIL PARTNERSHIP

You will have the opportunity to say a set form of words before you sign the schedule. You will need to bring with you at least two other people who are prepared to witness the registration and sign the civil partnership schedule.

Civil partnership registration is an entirely secular process, and the Civil Partnership Act prevents any religious service from taking place during the registration of a civil partnership. The Civil Partnership Act does not provide for a ceremony. Couples who wish to arrange for one at the time of registration should discuss this with the registration authority where the registration will be taking place when the initial arrangements are made.

LOCATION

Registry offices are civic departments and usually form part of town halls or other municipal buildings. Some registry offices have more than one room, so it's probably best to make a note of this before the big day. Many rooms are specifically designed with soft furnishings, appropriate décor and fresh flowers. A civil ceremony is usually much shorter than a traditional church wedding. Both parties have the choice of travelling to the reception (if relevant) together or separately. Many town halls have chamber rooms replete with stained glass windows, domed ceilings and even balconies, if you plan to invite a large group of guests. There will usually be at least one or two members of staff present to help with the proceedings. There are also usually less spacious annex rooms, if you wish to conduct a smaller ceremony.

GUESTS

Although technically the ceremony should take place 'with open doors' (that is, anyone who wants to witness the union can legally do so), a registry office cannot usually accommodate many people. Most people will accept the restrictions on numbers, and it might be easier to invite the bulk of the guests to the reception afterwards, in which case they should receive 'reception only' invitations.

TIMING

As the civil partnership ceremony will be fairly brief, it is highly likely that there will be several bookings in succession, particularly on a Saturday or on warm midsummer days. Be aware of this, and ensure that you 'get to the church on time' so to speak!

GIVING NOTICE OF YOUR CIVIL PARTNERSHIP

It is a legal requirement to give notice of your intention to register a civil partnership and, once given, your notices are publicised by the registration authority for a period of 15 days.

A civil partnership notice states for each person:
- Name and surname
- Date of birth
- Condition – marital or civil partnership status
- Occupation
- Nationality
- Place of formation

After giving notice, normally you must then wait 15 clear days before the civil partnership can be registered. For example, many people gave their notice on 5 December 2005, with their registration taking place on 21 December. This was the date that many couples across England and Wales made front page news with their unions. Once given, your notice is valid for 12 months. The minimum legal age for registering a civil partnership in England and Wales is 16, but written consent may be required for anyone under 18.

If you're subject to immigration controls, you will have to give notice of your intention to register a civil partnership at a designated office. But will not be able to do so unless:

- You have an entry clearance granted expressly for the purpose of registering a civil partnership in the UK. Entry clearance is the granting of permission to enter the UK by an Entry Clearance Officer in the British Embassy/High Commission in the person's country. It will usually be shown as a visa in the person's passport or travel document.

Or:
- You have the written permission of the Home Secretary to register a civil partnership in the UK. This will take the form of a certificate of approval, which can be obtained from the Immigration and Nationality Department. This will usually be issued where the person has been granted leave to enter or remain for over six months from the date on which they entered the UK and that leave is still in force. The certificate of approval will have to be

surrendered to the authorised person when notice is given.
Or:

• You fall within a class of persons specified by the Home Secretary. This will be someone with settled status in the UK or former spouses whose marriage has been annulled. These restrictions do not apply to foreign nationals who have been given the right of abode in the UK or who are exempt from immigration controls because of their employment. Authorised persons have a statutory duty to report any civil partnership they suspect has been registered for the sole purpose of evading statutory immigration controls.

SEARCHING FOR AN APPROVED VENUE

The List of Approved Premises is an easy-to use, straightforward reference source, which is found on the General Register Office. The directory is also available to order by phone. It lists all the locations that have been approved by registration authorities in England and Wales, and includes full details of addresses, contacts and approval expiry dates. This list is compiled on information provided by registration authorities, so strongly recommend you call your chosen venue to double check details and booking confirmations.

Make sure you and your partner have a thorough discussion about where you would like to host your ceremony, considering budget and the location of friends and family. Make sure the venue is accessible and has parking or public transport facilities to cater for your guests.

VOX-POP

Do you have any special vows you would like to say at your civil partnership?

Erica Jones, 35, nurse

'I would just like to say how much I love and adore her really. I hope that's not too sentimental!'

Meera Sekar, 38, nurse

'I feel the same, Erica has been a part of my life for eight years now so I would like to tell her I love her, plus maybe read out a poem or a love song.'

chapter 11

The Party

The party is the moment you can finally let off some steam! To make sure it goes without a hitch, check that there is a confirmed venue, that your guests are invited and there is enough alcohol to last through the day or night. From a logistical and budgeting perspective, these are the foundations of your party planning. The traditional wedding party is, of course, the stuff of comedic legend – drunk uncles, randy bridesmaids, vomiting children and Dad dancing to the 'Birdie Song'. You may have wonderfully sophisticated plans for your party (and the guests to live up to your intentions), but you cannot escape the fact that wedding parties tend to be an incredible social melting pot, as distant relatives, family and friends come together, perhaps for the first time. Naturally, the addition of alcohol to this mix can heat things up a tad – chuck on the flaming torch of your same-sex love and you might just see some explosions.

Being gay or lesbian, you're probably already adept at managing other people's clumsiness around the issue of your sexuality, but this is a time when a bit of careful preparation may be really handy. Your family and friends, for instance, may have very different ideas of what constitutes a party and some gentle massaging of expectations on both sides could help ensure there are no flashpoints. If your family's idea of a wedding party is a string quartet and cucumber sandwiches while your friends' is of banging party tunes and cocaine in the toilets, you might end up with some awkward moments. You'll have to draw up some parameters, but first you need to know who is coming to your party before making sure that everyone enjoys it, no matter how diverse their personal tastes may be.

A FAMILY AFFAIR

For some, the thought of organising a party with relatives involved sends a shiver to the spine. Families often argue and you may have the added stress of your partner's side being there, too; and of course, many gay and lesbian people consider their close-knit friendship group to be their adopted family. Many gay people have strained relations with parents and family, and it has been their friends who have been there through the hard times. So why should they be put the back of the queue just because of tradition? This could affect how you choose to carry out your celebrations. The ideal might be to throw a party that people from all walks of life enjoy together, but it might be safer to reach a happy medium by splitting the event into two sections.

AFTERNOON RECEPTION

Traditionally, the ceremony is followed by a reception at a nearby venue. On arrival the guests – family and friends of the bride and groom – will be offered a glass of champagne or sparkling wine accompanied by canapés or other nibbles. Typically, this will be followed by lunch or dinner, the cutting of the cake and the presentation of wedding gifts. You could do something completely different from this or cherry-pick the components that suit you and your budget. Either way, this is a relatively genteel occasion and you might find it easier on both your nerves and your budget to limit it to family and close friends.

EVENING CELEBRATIONS

You could have a second, larger invitation list that draws in your wider network of friends for the evening celebrations, which is where the fun begins. Potentially merrily imbibed, most relatives will want to hang around and gawp at the 'kids' (that's your thirty-something friends) careering around the dance-floor while dressed like Grammy award presenters on acid. Even if everyone stays together, you will find that separating into two will encourage some of the wilder guests to behave early on and then vice versa for the more restrained guests in the evening.

CHOOSING A VENUE

The second thing to consider if you have a large amount of guests attending the ceremony is the proximity from that venue to the party venue. Some places registered for civil partnerships are also able to host a party with a large crowd, but it's perfectly fine to have it in two separate venues. You may want to hold the party in a hotel or large hired house, so that guests from further afield only have to stagger upstairs to bed. This is a great way of having a hassle-free party with a touch of luxury. Conventional wedding protocol has it that parents of the happy couple foot the hotel bill, but if this isn't possible many guests will be happy to pay for their own room, provided you make it clear from the start. The venue, like the rest of your plans, doesn't have to follow tradition. If a luxury pastel coloured hotel is your idea of hell, you may want to think of somewhere with a bit more imagination. There's nothing like a quirky or eccentric venue to bring that special moment alive for your celebrations, while reflecting your personality and even sense of humour.

top tips for an unusual venue

For something out of the ordinary, there are so many options! Do remember that budget plays a big part, though: the more unusual and exotic, the more likely it is to be expensive. Remember, too, that you need the right number of guests to make a venue work, so for a small, intimate gathering, a ballroom is probably not top of the list!

Here's just a few ideas with some examples so you can visit their websites and see the kind of thing this type of venue offers. You can then get on the internet and investigate what's available in your location.

- **A boat:** From modern motor launches to traditional tall ships, you can get married on board a ship, even arranging for Tower Bridge to open up for you. For example: www.topchart.co.uk
- **A castle or historic building:** Try somewhere such as The Atrium in Edinburgh. Registered for ceremonies, this modern and atmospheric venue is at the foot of Edinburgh Castle. The space takes on a cathedral-like atmosphere, ideal for those who would like to capture the romance of a church for their ceremony while having a top restaurant on hand for the reception. For example: www.atriumrestaurant.co.uk
- **A country manor or country house:** How about having a posh party in a Victorian stately home? For example, Orchardleigh House in Somerset boasts 300 acres of parkland and lakes, and inside a band and disco until dawn. This venue can accommodate up to 90 guests. For example: www.orchardleigh.net
- **A hotel or a bar:** If you're really in the party mood, you can hold your civil partnership ceremony and your party at a bar such as the stylish Bar Fibre in Leeds. This venue can arrange everything from catering to décor, and even the fancy car that gets you there. For example: www.clubmission.com

- **A marquee:** If you are having the party at home and have a decent-sized garden, then a marquee is a must-have option for wedding-like celebrations. Even if you're not holding it at home, if the venue has grounds, then professional people can be hired to set up all sizes of marquees to fit large and small numbers, be it a ceremony at Skegness or Skibo Castle. For example: www.fieldandlawn.com

- **A top restaurant:** There are beautiful restaurants all over the UK and many are now registered for ceremonies. Soho House has three spacious rooms for hire and a capacity of 80 for the ceremony (50 seated, 30 standing). Located in the heart of Soho, it includes a roof terrace with retractable roof. Licensed until 3.00 am on Saturdays. For example: www.sohohouse21.com/weddings

- **A museum, gallery, theatre or arts venue:** Any of these can provide an unusual setting if you are interested in the arts or have other specific hobbies or interests. For example: www.canalmuseum.org.uk

- **A spa:** Lythe Hill Hotel & Spa in Surrey is just one example. A charming country hotel with 41 bedrooms and suites, with a new health and beauty spa able to provide a relaxing and soothing element to your day. Licensed for civil ceremonies for up 125 people. For example: www.lythehill.co.uk

- **A sports venue:** If you are a sports fan, you'll find that some sports clubs are now licensed premises. Tottenham Hotspur fans, for example, are in luck! For example: www.haringey.gov.uk

- **A waterside setting:** This can be a most romantic location, although you'll need good weather to make the most of the outdoors. Fortunately, many venues have a conservatory so you don't have to worry about the British weather letting you down. For example: www.themill-hotel.co.uk

VENUE CHECKLIST

There's a lot to think about, so use a checklist to record details of what needs doing and what's been done.

Venue details	
Address	
Tel	
Fax	
E-mail	
Reception location	
Contact name	
Address	
Tel	
Fax	
E-mail	
Room size(s)	
Furniture	
Decorations	
Heating	
Cloakroom facilities	
Changing facilities	
Parking	
Gift display area	
Dancing/entertainment	
Licensing arrangements	
Insurance	
Deposit paid	
Balance due date	

SEATING PLAN

If you're having a sit-down meal, an overall seating plan is usually prepared so that guests know the general position of their seats as they enter the dining room. Only you know the pecking order of your guests, but you might want to take your lead from a conventional heterosexual wedding. The top table comprises the happy couple with their parents and attendants. Other family members are seated on tables closest to the top table, then friends, work colleagues and other more distant acquaintances. Staff at your chosen venue will probably be able to advise you on the best arrangement of tables to ensure that everyone has a good view of you and your partner (and you of all of them), can hear the speeches and so on. A traditional top table is shown here:

Best man	Groom's father	Bride's mother	Groom	Bride	Bride's father	Groom's mother	Chief bridesmaid

Obviously, with a civil partnership you can be more flexible. The most important thing is to maintain harmony amongst all the interested parties.

CATERING

 A well fed guest is a happy guest! You don't want to be worrying about any last-minute mishaps in the kitchen, so take your time picking a reliable caterer. Many companies offer a full-service civil partnership planner, allowing the busy couple a variety of service options for their memorable day. Combined with the right music, delicious food and, of course, a decadent wedding cake, catering can really set the standard for a day that will live long in everyone's hearts.

There are numerous ways to organise the catering for your civil partnership celebrations ranging from a finger food buffet in your home to a full sit-down meal at a hired restaurant or venue. Do you want a sit down meal or buffet? What time of day are you going to be eating? This might affect the style of food you order and you need to consider how hungry your guests will be before deciding when to serve each meal. Bear in mind, too, that if your guests bring children there could be tantrums if they're kept hungry.

 top tip for floral art

When you are serving up food, try to order a few extra flowers that are the flower of choice for your civil partnership and use them as decoration on the food platters.

Choosing a caterer

Professional caterers offer an incredible range of food services, though all differing at price. Of course you could always plead with Gordon Ramsay for a discount! Failing that, go for a caterer that has been personally recommended and ask for references, if appropriate.

Get a few comparable quotations. Most cater on a per-head price based on the meal, but find out whether the wine is included in the package or whether there is a charge for corkage. Make sure, too, that the cost includes clearing it all up. You will be required to place a booking deposit, then pay the balance and confirm final numbers at an agreed date. Confirm all agreements in writing, including details of deposits and final payment terms. It is unwise to settle in full beforehand in case there is any disagreement over the provision of services.

CATERING PHRASES

- **Buffet:** Guests help themselves from large displays of food. This is a great way to offer a variety of dishes and allow guests to pick and choose.
- **Cocktail reception:** This elegant type of reception usually runs from around 4 to 7 pm and features extensive hors d'oeuvres or a light buffet.
- **Consumption bar:** The bartenders keep a running tab, and you pay the final bill at the end of the evening, based on how much your guests drank. A good idea if your guests are light drinkers.
- **Entrée:** The main course of your reception meal.
- **Food platters:** Large serving dishes of food are placed at each table and guests pass them around and serve themselves.
- **Food stations:** Similar to buffet service in that guests serve themselves, but instead of one long table, food is divided into several themed locations, such as a pasta or seafood table.
- **French service:** No, your waiters will not have a sprig of garlic when they serve your meal! Instead, expect waiters to serve each guest individually from a tray held by another waiter.
- **Gratuity:** The tip. Caterers usually include this 20 per cent fee in their final tally.
- **Mixed drinks:** Drinks that require more than one ingredient or special mixing equipment. Providing them at your reception could raise the bar tab.
- **Open bar:** You pay a flat fee for your guests to drink all night.

- **Plated service:** The plates are already full of food when they're brought from the kitchen and placed in front of your seated guests.
- **Poured drinks:** Easy-to-make drinks, those beverages with only one ingredient and that aren't shaken or stirred.
- **Russian service:** Similar to French service. The extremely co-ordinated waiters hold the trays of food in one hand and serve the guests with the other. Also known as silver service.
- **Tray/butlered service:** Waiters walk among your guests with trays of hors d'oeuvres or drinks.

Self-catering

If you are choosing this option, you are either a) a culinary expert, b) hard up for cash, or c) mad. Jokes aside, think very carefully about catering for your own party. It is a lot of hard work both immediately before and on the day of ceremony. You might prefer to spend the day on other things – like soaking up the fact that you are now legally bound. Or just soaking up the booze.

Most people who cater for their own wedding choose a buffet. It is usually only practical to serve cold food. That way you can create a menu that you can prepare in advance and freeze. Get help with the preparation from friends and have someone else serve the food on the day itself.

If food is not a priority and you don't intend to lay out a huge platter of chicken wings, it is best to stick with stylish nibbles. Get creative with quails eggs and celery salt, field mushroom and hollandaise tartlets, king prawn and mangetout skewers, or rare roast beef with wholegrain mustard and crème fraîche. It's the small things that count and these have the ability to say more about your taste than anything else.

Wedding cake

Although the wedding cake is usually one of the last details couples settle on before the big day, it's just as important for setting the tone and style of the celebration as the flowers or the invitations. An elegant, towering croquembouche studded with golden almonds and wrapped in clouds of spun sugar sends a different message from a rich gianduja truffle cake decorated with fresh fruit and dusted with gold powder or a white chocolate satin apricot cake adorned with flowers. A wedding cake should reflect the tastes, beliefs, and desires of the couple, so have a good think before you decide!

top tip for cakes

A traditional fruit wedding cake is usually served in 2.5 cm (1 in) square pieces. Square cakes are better value than other shapes and are easier to cut.

DID YOU KNOW?

Cakes have played a part of weddings throughout history. The Romans shared a plain cake of flour, salt and water during the wedding ceremony itself, as Native Americans still do today.

Drinks

Alcohol is likely to play an integral role into getting the party started and the sooner you realise it the better. The arrangements for the bar will vary tremendously, depending on the style of your reception, but the right variety and quantity of drinks is important. Don't forget soft drinks.

Guests are often offered a sherry or glass of champagne on arrival. Wines or sparkling wines tend to be served with the meal, with wine, beer or spirits later in the evening. But why not try some new liquor or introduce a rare but favourite drink of your own to your guests? As the evening closes in, bring out the exotic cocktails and tequila slammers.

VOX-POP

What type of food would you like to serve at your reception?

Lily Austin, 36, skiing instructor

'Just something for everyone really, I think I'd be most inclined to have a buffet with veggie dishes, as I don't eat meat but will eat fish.'

Isabella McNair, 25, snowboarder

'I think I'd go for Italian food, like a nice tagliatelle with pesto sauce and tomatoes.'

Catering Checklist

Caterer information
Company
Contact name
Address
Tel
Fax
E-mail
Number of serving staff
Provision of crockery and cutlery
Agreed menu
Deposit paid
Balance due date
Self-catering information
Choose menu
Name of catering equipment hire company
Address
Tel
Fax
E-mail
Baking equipment
Crockery
Cutlery
Table linen
Serving dishes
Date for delivery
Date for return
Drinks checklist
Bar to be provided by
Choice of drinks
When drinks are to be served
Bar staff
Drinks to be obtained from
Address
Tel
Fax

E-mail
Quantities and drinks ordered
Sale or return
Glasses to be obtained from
Deposit paid
Balance due date
Type and number of glasses hired
Return date for glasses
Spirit measures, optics, ice buckets
Bottle openers, corkscrews
Water jugs and glasses
Coffee and tea-making arrangements

Licensing laws are strict in the UK and hotels or club premises will have their own licence. If all the drinks are to be dispensed free, you do not require a licence, but you will if you intend to have a cash bar, whether your guests are paying for the drinks or you are putting an amount behind the bar.

Be a true socialite and have staff at your party. You won't enjoy serving up drinks yourself or seeing everybody frantically pouring their own drinks. Most venues will employ their own staff, so put this on the priority list of things to ask when looking for a venue.

DÉCOR FOR THE RECEPTION

You'll need to start thinking about décor and centrepiece ideas for tables, although we would strongly advise you not to go with bowls of flowers and floating candles, or anything similarly nauseating. Traditional weddings are full of large silk floral blooms immersed in glass bowls, so be inspired for your own party. Try basing everything around a colour scheme such as all white or turn your party into a black and white ball.

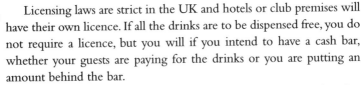

top tip for flowers

A florist should be given approximately four months' notice in advance of your party.

Glorious flowers

We're not suggesting you go out and spend a Sir Elton John amount of just under £300,000 on flowers, but they are an essential element to the event as a whole. Unless you want your floral displays to be very simple, it's wise to have them professionally prepared. Seek personal recommendations from friends and ask to see if they have prepared flowers for other weddings to see the quality of their work. You might want the colour co-ordination to reflect what you're wearing or if you had an overall theme in mind.

Confetti

You've got a lot of choices for this traditional decorative touch: gold dots, gold hearts, clear hearts, iridescent hearts, assorted mini stars, gold horseshoes and hearts, pearl-white hearts, love hearts hollow, love with gold hearts, just married silver, multicoloured foil star-shaped, musical notes, red and silver hearts, red dots, royal blue, and multicoloured heart-shaped confetti. Some venues and registry offices have strict rules about what can be thrown and where, so check before you order and warn your guests about any restrictions that might be imposed.

ENTERTAINMENT

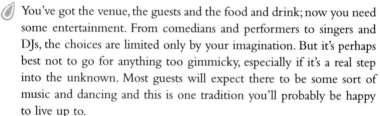 You've got the venue, the guests and the food and drink; now you need some entertainment. From comedians and performers to singers and DJs, the choices are limited only by your imagination. But it's perhaps best not to go for anything too gimmicky, especially if it's a real step into the unknown. Most guests will expect there to be some sort of music and dancing and this is one tradition you'll probably be happy to live up to.

Consider the following:

- Band
- Burlesque performers
- Comedian
- DJ
- Function band
- Harpists
- Line/country dancing
- Live jazz band
- String quartets
- Tribute bands
- Wedding singer

Music

Don't underestimate the importance of music. Your options start from CDs or MP3 player connected to a PA system to hiring a live band to perform. The latter is usually a winning idea, provided that their chosen sound is reasonably inclusive. You might also want to get up on stage and serenade your partner with a Cher torch song or two, but be prepared for the party to turn into an unusually well-dressed karaoke-fest. There are a lot of tribute bands that favour the gay market. These are all well and good for trashy cabaret nights and that time you saw them at Mardi Gras, but have a good think about how sophisticated and inclusive you want the mood to be. If you always thought the 'Birdie Song' would be appropriate to walk down the aisle to, you might well enjoy some of the *Ab Fab* impersonators and Abba tributes that are readily available to the pink pound.

Most of you will have songs that have made you dance, laugh and cry all at the same time. You may want these to soundtrack this special event effectively. The simplest route to take is to a hire a DJ (which is where it all seems to start adding up!) although what is not so simple is choosing a set list. On one hand you may have your dance queens who will expect some house tunes, whilst on the other you'll have your middle of the road wonders wanting to slow dance to Celine Dion every five minutes. The best way to do it is to cater for all by starting off slow and progressing through the evening. The DJ will, of course, know how to handle it, but it is a good idea to make a song list of all the party favourites and camp classics you want to hear on the night.

top tip for lighting

Good lighting is a huge encouragement for people to get up, dance and have a good time. You can make the dance floor spin with the various different lighting effects that are available for hire. You might want to create the atmosphere of your very own underground club with colour changing panels, glitter balls and a revolving dance floor... yes, you too can turn your wedding video into a Kylie promo! This may blow a big hole in your wallet, but you can at least get something of the mood with the house-lights switched off and a few cheap spinning light globes around the room.

🌢 JUST SAY NO?

Drugs are an issue you might have to discuss when it comes to the party. If you or your friends are recreational drug users, do you want to partake at your wedding party? If you'd rather ditch the drugs, are you going to ask your friends to do the same? If drugs are likely to be taken at the party, is usage going to be responsible, given that children and relatives may be present? Are you willing to risk arrest at your own wedding party? All this might also affect your decision to separate the celebration into two parts.

Entertainment checklist

DJ/musicians	
Name	
Address	
Tel	
Fax	
E-mail	
Date booked	
Time to start	
Time to finish	
Background music during the meal	
Range of music requested	
First dance	
Special requests	

GOOD TIMES

The last bit of advice is to enjoy it! Don't get caught up in any drama; your friends will be on hand to deal with that. Don't be worried about families; it may be the first time your dad has seen you kiss your partner, and it may be the first time for the rest of your family, but it's something they will just have to get over. This night is your night. You don't have to apologise for anything. You will be civil partners, so don't let anything come between you!

Celebrity wedding

David and Victoria Beckham hired singer Beverley Knight for their wedding party to sing her own songs and soul favourites. You could always go one poorer and hire your local pub singer.

VOX-POP

Terry, 62, and Patrick, 49, London

'Our civil partnership meant a lot to us, especially after being together for over 25 years. We celebrated by hiring a riverboat along the Thames starting from Richmond where we had the ceremony. We are of a certain age where getting sloshed or going to a club just isn't appropriate for us. We also have our guests to think of. Though some are young and probably wanted to get on to dry land and into a disco, it was our day and they respected that. Remember that your friends will most likely go with the flow and never complain on a day like this, if they do then they're not much of a friend! The party was fabulous with food and live music throughout the day. The only advice we can give from our experience is have it exactly as you want it. Your guests will enjoy it if you are enjoying it.'

chapter 12

The Speeches

'Brevity is the best recommendation of speech, whether in a senator or an orator.' Marcus Tullius Cicero

At traditional wedding receptions, the speeches and toasts take place after guests have finished their meal and usually occur before the cutting of the cake. In heterosexual unions, the bride is rarely required to make a speech, but in the case of civil partnerships it will be up to both you and your partner to decide on the order of speeches. You will have to decide if one or both of you will speak, and also think about which parental figures will say a few words, depending on who is there. Speaking from personal experience, these speeches can often be a daunting and sometimes terrifying prospect. However, here is an easy, straightforward guide to tackling speeches.

BACKGROUND

If you decide you want to make a full-blown speech, you will want to wow your audience and have them laughing in the right places for the right reasons. To achieve this, it is crucial that you prepare carefully and methodically. Professional speakers use a set of skills known as the three Ps: preparation; practice; performance.

Preparation

Even politicians who are greatly experienced in taking the floor and addressing large groups of people need to prepare in advance. We would advise against an impromptu, off-the-cuff speech. You should have at least a vague idea of the content you wish to use.

The preparation stage is the part of the process that demands the most work. If you plot the foundations of a building sturdily, then the tower will be strong and well rooted. The same applies to a speech. Without thorough preparation and good material, it is hard to deliver a good speech, even if you practise 100 times in front of the mirror.

Great speeches have the capacity to transcend their initial purpose directed at any given audience.

Decide how to prepare your material

You can either use entirely your own material or jump online for some pointers, even if you're familiar with making speeches. Many websites or specialist books provide ready-made speeches that you can use as they stand or make more personal by mixing and matching several examples and adding some of your own jokes and anecdotes.

Length of speech

As the great Roman orator Cicero said, brevity is a good rule of thumb. Five minutes is about the right length of time to be speaking. It may seem like an eternity to you, but will be long enough to get across everything you want to say without losing your audience (particularly if you have youngsters present who have a short attention span). A well-versed and debonair rhetorical genius might want to extend this to 10 minutes.

Choose your subject wisely

You only need one novel idea to make your speech successful and memorable. When coming up with a suitable theme, be aware of the comic values of the audience and take care not to offend the guests. The content of the speech should, in some way, reflect the widely known history of the couple or their families. You also need to grab the attention of the guests and involve them so they can anticipate the story outcome. However, a surprising or witty punch line to rouse the crowd with laughter is a great way to accentuate their enjoyment. Make the point lucidly and don't try to cram 10 facts into one story. If you feel unable to come up with such an idea, don't worry! Instead, use a combination of ideas, stories, jokes and quotations and meld them together to achieve a similar ending.

top tip for speech writing

If in doubt, leave it out! Don't mention former partnerships and spare your partner's their blushes by avoiding digging up any unnecessary drama!

The point of the speech is to entertain, rather than to shock or offend.

- Banish stereotypes. Lesbians have buzz cuts and gay men wear tiaras. Not in the 21st Century, so cast away any blanket generalisations!
- Do not make derogatory remarks or highlight regrets. Anything that might make your partner or either family appear foolish automatically makes you look silly for raising the subject. Whether you find it amusing isn't really the point. Snubs or negative comments are sure to put a damper on the day and may upset the couple. Maintain a balanced sense of judgement.
- Avoid rude jokes or sexual innuendos unless you are 100 per cent sure that all the guests will laugh and find your allusions amusing. As always, bear in mind older and younger generations, for whom this may be their first civil partnership.
- Get someone to double-check your speech for unintentional double meanings and puns. It is always a good plan to get a second opinion from someone you trust, perhaps a mutual friend.

 ## top tips for jokes

Instead of typical wedding jokes, which tend to focus on the battle of the sexes, here are some gay and lesbian-specific jokes. Just make sure they are used in the right context!

Lesbian humour
Q: What can two femmes do in bed?
A: Each other's makeup.

Q: What kind of humour do lesbians like?
A: Tongue in cheek.

Q: Why do lesbians like to have gay male friends?
A: Someone has to do the cooking!

Q: What drives a lesbian up the wall?
A: A crack in the ceiling.

Gay humour

What a drag it is getting old...

When I went to the bar tonight, I noticed this old boy sitting all alone in the corner and he was crying over his cocktail.

I stopped and asked him what was wrong.

He said: 'I have a 22 year old lover at home. I met him a month or so ago, right here in this very bar!' He continued: 'He makes love to me every morning and then he makes me pancakes, sausage, fresh fruit and freshly ground, brewed coffee.'

I said: 'Well, then why are you crying?'

He said: 'He makes me homemade soup for lunch and my favourite brownies and then he makes love to me half the afternoon.'

I said: 'Well, so why are you crying?'

He said: 'For dinner he makes me a gourmet meal with wine and my favourite dessert and then he makes love to me until 2:00 am.'

I said: 'Well, for goodness' sake! Why in the world would you be CRYING!'

And he said: 'I CAN'T REMEMBER WHERE I LIVE!'

Q: Why do gay men like to have lesbian friends?
A: Someone has to mow the lawn.

The perfect man loves cooking
Cleaning and vacuuming too
He'll do anything in his power
To convey his love to you.

He will never make you cry
Or hurt you in any way
To hell with this stupid poem
The perfect man is gay!

Speaker's notes

Your speech should draw attention to yourself and consist of a steady stream of words. However, unless you have a photographic memory, you will need help in remembering everything you want to say. Flapping, unruly bits of paper will not aid your cause.

An A5 card will be less distracting than a big sheet of A4 paper. You may also need to consider the venue location, as a flimsy piece of paper won't hold up against a blustery breeze if you are outside.

You may prefer to use the smaller postcard sized Post-It notes, which can be hidden in the palm of your hand. However, you will need more of them, and it may be tricky to keep your place as you conduct the speech.

During the design and initial stages of practising, you may change the wording and content several times. If you type or word-process your speech, you can make alterations more easily and change any headings if necessary. When the content is settled, the words can be transferred to the A5 cards.

However, there is no need to cram the speech on to as few cards as possible. The writing may be illegible and leave you confused and unsure of your place, so use abbreviations and shorthand to maximise space on every card. Highlight, emphasise and underline key words and phrases. It's also a good idea to number the cards, just in case you drop them. Alternatively punch holes in them and connect them with a tag or key ring.

Practice

We're sure you've lots of experience of sitting in front of your childhood mirror crooning to your favourite diva. Revisit that technique now; or you might want to record yourself, to hear how your delivery sounds.

Rhythm

The way a speech is spoken is crucial to its execution. Avoid sounding pompous or patronising on delivery, and make sure you maintain a steady sense of rhythm, using intonations at the end of any questions. Remember to speak the speech; don't read it in a dreary, monotonous manner. Deliver it as if you are talking in conversation and modulate your voice up and down. Remember that the larger the audience, the greater the modulation needed.

An important prerequisite to any speech is the ability to recite a cracking joke with conviction, so make sure you rehearse any comic moment thoroughly. However, let the audience laugh and try to resist bursting into a fit of giggles yourself as it may put you off kilter for the remaining oration. Sound the joke out to your friends, and make sure you get a universal nod of approval.

Once you are satisfied with your delivery during practice, you may find it useful to put headings in appropriate places on your cue cards. Make these headings large and bold. It is then easier to find your place if you do need to refer to the cards, and easier to spot the next subject.

Practise making eye contact with your audience (see below). You must be sure your voice will be heard; otherwise there is no point in making a speech at all. The technique of using a microphone must be practised, so have a run-through or seek out the advice of an experienced user.

Last minute hitches?

It is important to visualise how you will effortlessly recover from any little problems that may occur on the day. If you spill your drink, step back, cover the drink with your napkin, apologise to the person sitting next to you and ask for their help. Then turn back to the guests and think of a witty punch line: 'Well, I knew I had to do something dramatic to get started!' Practise for every eventuality and make sure there is someone on hand to help if the equipment misbehaves.

Performance

Eye contact

Try not to have your eyes glued to your card. Read a phrase, look up and make eye contact, deliver it and look down for the next phrase. If you make a point of establishing eye contact with a different section of the audience each time, by the end of the speech you will have looked at and included everyone.

Being heard

Don't try to compete with extraneous noise. When you are about to start speaking, many people will be in free-flowing conversation and glasses may be clinking, so be sure to wait until the noise has died down before beginning. When the room has quietened down, perhaps throw in a witty phrase to entice to audience and get the show on the road!

ORDER OF THE SPEECHES

In conventional wedding etiquette, the first speech is generally given by the father of the bride, followed by the groom, who replies on behalf of himself and his new wife, and includes giving thanks to the bridesmaids. Then the best man replies on behalf of the bridesmaids; and then launches into what is generally expected to be something of a comedy turn. Take or leave elements of this, depending on your tastes and the style of your reception.

'Father of the bride'

The first speech is normally made by the bride's father, but of course in a civil partnership, you and your partner will have to decide who will be making this speech. An older relative can also make a speech if necessary. The specific content is obviously dependent on the nature of the relationship, but is usually semi-serious in tone and will include four or five important elements:

- The speaker should praise his son or daughter and highlight the happiness that he has had in seeing his child grow up into a beautiful adult. A brief anecdote or short story relating to their early life may be an appropriate opener.
- Congratulations should be given to the other partner and joy expressed at the union, on behalf on the entire family (if present). He should welcome all other parties into his family.
- The speaker should express his confidence in the couple's future together and wish them a long and prosperous life together. Maybe he could offer some pearls of wisdom relating to his own experiences.
- He should also add how happy and proud he is to see his son or daughter in a civil partnership, and will ask the guests to join him in wishing them well.
- The toast to the bride and groom is usually made at the end of the speech, which should be made to 'the happy couple'. This part of the speech will need careful practising, as it is crucial to be clear and concise here.

The 'groom's' reply

At heterosexual weddings, the groom replies to the toast and on behalf of his wife and himself, and makes around seven or eight important points, lasting for no more than five minutes. In civil partnerships, you and your partner will have to decide who makes the speech. Its primary function is to thank and acknowledge everyone who has helped you. Here are some basic points to include:

- Thank the father for the toast he has just proposed.
- Express happiness and say how fortunate you are to be joining your partner's family. You might also choose to add a few words on your romantic history, or your future intentions to secure your partner's happiness later in life.

- Thank your or your partner's parents for hosting the occasion, if relevant.
- Thank your own parents for their care, affection and diligence in taking care of you in your childhood.
- You might want to respond to any advice given from the previous speech. This is the chance for a more off-the-cuff or impromptu remark if something witty or relevant comes to mind.
- Mention what a pleasure and honour it is to see so many friends and family in attendance. Of course, this is dependent on the size of the reception.
- Make special mention of anyone who made a noteworthy contribution to the day, for example an aunt who made the canapés. Any regret about absent guests should be added here.
- Throw in a complimentary remark about the beauty and efficiency of any bridesmaids and attendants present, particularly the best man and/or matron of honour. This is the point at which to give out any thank-you gifts, if this has not already been done.
- Finally, propose a toast to the bridesmaids, if applicable. The toast may be 'to the bridesmaids' or you can use their first names. If there are no bridesmaids, make a toast to your partner.

The 'best man'

Of all the traditional speeches at a wedding reception, the best man's is the most anticipated and your civil partnership will be no exception! Guests look for humour from all the speeches, and are usually happy to reward even the feeblest attempt at a joke with a torrent of booming laughter. It is the role of the best man to do his best to put on a bit of a show and raise a few chuckles.

Actually, this is not as daunting as it sounds. The best man usually speaks last, by which time guests tend to have relaxed considerably, a fact perhaps connected to the rapid consumption of wine and an assorted concoction of beverages! By this time, the guests' sense of humour threshold will have lowered considerably, so anything that vaguely sounds like a punch line should bring the house down.

Another advantage a best man will have at this point is familiarity. Unless you're having a very formal occasion with a separate Master of Ceremonies, the best man has been acting as the host or anchorman of the whole occasion, so he will be a widely recognisable figure at the event. Here are some basic points you might want to pass on to your best man or equivalent:

- The traditional best man's beginning often involves thanking both partners for their gifts. It is also customary to compliment the bridesmaids, if present, and the other attendants.
- To draw in the audience, it is a good idea to tell some behind-the-scenes stories about preparing for the civil partnership, especially any amusing incidents occurred or narrowly averted disasters.
- You can also make a point of addressing the couple, and especially of talking to your close friend who is getting hitched.
- The traditional main task of this type of speech is to embarrass your friend, whether the 'groom' or the 'bride'. Your material should be funny without being nasty and excessively risqué. Props can be used here (although perhaps leave the dildo at home), and stories perhaps pertaining to any stag or hen nights often crop up.
- Balance the mockery with some sincerity. Talk about how you met and how you came to be such close friends. Include how much you really think of him or her, your perspective on the growing relationship between both parties and your best wishes for their future life together.
- Your other duties consist of reading any telegrams and other messages from invited guests unable to attend the civil partnership after your main speech.
- Conclude with a toast to the happy couple.

VOX-POP

What would you include in your civil partnership speech?

Maggie Staples, 42, hairdresser

'I'd definitely like to thank everyone who showed up on my special day and made me feel loved!'

Angie Benson, 39, stylist

'Not sure how drunk I'd be by that stage. Maybe it's better that Maggie does the talking!'

top tips for quotations

Here are some useful quotations you may like to use in your speech, but remember not to overdo it.

- 'Love makes the world go round. She who has never lov'd, has never liv'd.'

  John Gay

- 'The course of true love never did run smooth.'

  William Shakespeare

- 'If male homosexuals are called 'gay,' then female homosexuals should be called 'ecstatic.''

  Roberts' Rules of Lesbian Living, Shelly Roberts

- 'A wise man makes more opportunities than he finds.'

  Francis Bacon

- 'Marriage is the one subject on which all women agree and all men disagree.'

  Oscar Wilde

- 'Love is like quicksilver in the hand. Leave the fingers open, and it stays. Clutch it, and it darts away.'

  Dorothy Parker

chapter 13

Capturing Your Memories

The couple that do not want images to remind them of their big day are rare, and will likely come to regret the decision – as will those who don't make sensible preparations. While many will have a friend armed with a digital camera who considers themselves the next Mario Testino, it is advised that you hire a professional with plenty of wedding photography experience to capture your day. The less than happy (OK, plain sad) couple who entrusted their wedding day shots to someone who got drunk and lost the camera are not as uncommon as you might think. Family and friends who do manage to make it through the day with their cameras intact will no doubt provide plenty of additional, if wonky, snapshots for the album, but a professional will ensure you cover a full range of shots – such as the exchange of rings, the couple with family – and will guarantee to deliver them. What is most important is that you end up with a set of images you can treasure for life. An experienced professional will not only know how to avoid annoyances, such as stray children on the edge of frame, but will also help the awkward and unphotogenic look their best. Though many would prefer to hire a gay and lesbian or gay-friendly photographer – and certainly an unsympathetic homophobe would be a disaster – you should ensure that whoever does your photographs is reputable. It's more important that they know how to focus a camera than all the words to 'Somewhere Over The Rainbow'.

You may also consider a videographer to produce a record of your day. A video of your day will almost certainly cost more than straightforward photography and it is likely that video will be in addition to photographs. Do not attempt to cut corners by extracting still images from any video footage, as it is unlikely to be of satisfactory quality. Costs for both photography and video will depend on variables such as how extensive you wish coverage to be – for instance, simply the ceremony or the preparations and reception, too – and the delivery format – prints, CD-Rom or DVDs for all your friends and family. The checklists at the end of this chapter (see page 131) will help you decide what is essential to you and what type of coverage is a luxury so that you can manage your budget.

Once you have your images, you might want to incorporate them in a website that can easily be accessed by friends and family. If you have a home internet connection, check to see whether your Internet Service Provider (ISP) offers free storage space for you to build a site as part of your monthly service charge. Building a basic site that includes text and photographs and even video content is simpler than many think and plenty of ISPs offer step-by-step guidance. However, for quick and slick results you may want to pay a professional. Search the internet for local website designers and compare costs and examples of their work. It's up to you how inventive your site is, but clean, simple and straightforward is never out of fashion. Animated rainbow flags accompanied by tinny Muzak on the other hand...

CHOOSING A PHOTOGRAPHER

Make sure your wedding photographer is a member of a reputable association such as The Master Photographers' Association or The British Institute of Professional Photography and that their specialist area is wedding photography. If you are insistent on using a gay or lesbian photographer who is not a member of the above organisations, then be even more stringent with your checks.

Check potential photographers' portfolios. Most will have websites so this should be simple. Photographs should be sharp and clear and not catch people in awkward poses. Check that there is a back-up photographer and equipment in case of last minute illness or emergencies. Establish who owns the copyright and negatives.

Most photographers offer a wedding package, which includes the photographer's attendance to take a specified number of photographs plus delivering a CD-ROM of shots and an album of about twenty printed photographs. Be very specific about what you will receive as prints are expensive. Alternatively, there may be an attendance fee and a price per print and album. They may also have a package for parents' albums with a standard charge for prints.

Proofs are not usually available for the reception, but with most wedding photographer's now using digital equipment you should be able to get some idea of your best shots. Determine with the photographer exactly when your final images will delivered, be they in print or 'soft' (digital) form. Check what the charge will be for proofs, whether they will be over-stamped and whether you can keep them. Some photographers insist that you view the proofs at their studio. This may be inconvenient for you or your guests.

Discuss the style you want, referring to the portfolio, and any special shots you would like. If you are flying off in a hot air balloon for example, you may want this to be recorded. There are many different specialist styles from formal to documentary. Don't be afraid to ask questions or point out your likes and dislikes.

Photographers do not usually attend the reception. If you want them to attend, you must make special arrangements.

At the point of booking, confirm dates and times in writing. Agree the fees, again, in writing, and pay the deposit in good time to secure your photographer. Agree final payment arrangements.

top tip: how do I look?

With the plans in place for capturing of your day, it's worth taking a little time to consider how you'll come across. Many people hate the sight of themselves in photographs. From nervous pouts to stiff smiles, often we don't do ourselves any favours! Take a tip from the celebrities and put in a little practice. By taking pictures of yourselves at home, you'll get a better idea of how to look relaxed on camera. But once in the hands of your wedding photographer, let him or her do the directing.

IF YOU CAN'T AFFORD A PHOTOGRAPHER

It's best to hire a professional photographer for the day but if you're really strapped, then arrange for a competent and sober friend or relative to take the key shots using a digital camera, ideally with four mega pixel capacity or more. Try to take most of the pictures outside in good natural light. Position yourselves so the sun is behind the photographer. Unless it's overcast, midday tends to be the least flattering time for photographs, late afternoon the most kind to the face. Your photographer should mount a digital camera on a tripod and set the image size to the highest possible setting for the greatest quality. The bigger the image size, the larger the prints you'll be able to have made at a high street photographic developer. Check you're happy with each image before letting people move on.

PHOTOGRAPHY CHECKLISTS

Here you will find a comprehensive checklist of the photographs you'll probably want to have. Tick the shots you feel are essential and agree these and the total, final costs with the photographer in writing. You can personalise the list to make sure you get exactly what you want for your ceremony, but agree it with the photographers, otherwise they might go off and do their own 'arty' conceptual view of your day! Outline clearly the style and composition you are looking for throughout all the photos.

At home

Close-up of partners	
Full length of partners	
Partners with their mothers	
Partners with his fathers	
Partners with parents	
Partners with their family	
Partners with friends/best man	
Partners and all attendants	

Before the ceremony

First partner	
Second partner	
Parents	
Friends	
Partners with family and friends	
Guests arriving	
The party assembled	

During the ceremony

Exchange of rings	
Signing the register	
Displays of affection	

After the ceremony

Partners leaving the registry office	
Partners together	
First partner with own family	
Second partner with own family	
First partner with own friends	
Second partner with own friends	
First partner's family group photo	
Second partner's family group photo	
Guests throwing confetti	
Both partners with full party	

At the reception

Partners arriving	
Partners receiving guests	
Partners with respective parents	
Partners with special friends	
Party members during the speeches	
Partners cutting their cake	
Partners dancing the first dance	
Musicians or entertainers	
Partners leaving for the honeymoon	
The going-away car	

Photographer information

Name	
Address	
Tel	
E-mail	
Dates confirmed	
Times of attendance	
Package:	
Number of photographs to be taken	
Number of prints allowed	
Style of album	
Proofs included	
Cost	
Parents' albums:	
Number of prints allowed	
Style of album	
Cost	
Date for proofs	
Date for photograph order	
Date for provision of photographs	
Total cost	
Deposit paid	
Balance due date	

Celebrity wedding

Kate Moss invited Mario Testino to take pictures of her planned wedding to rocker Pete Doherty. Their wedding didn't take place though, so Mario may still have a gap in his diary...

Guests' photograph orders

Name	
Address	
Telephone	
Proof number	
Quantity	
Cost	
Paid	

VOX-POP

David, 29, and Bruce, 33, West Dunbartonshire

'We enquired with a local wedding photography service. We were a bit hesitant at first as we were pretty sure this would be the first same-sex couple to have asked so soon after civil partnerships being made law, but to our surprise they had a very encouraging attitude. They even offered us a discount, though we were not sure if we should be happy or offended by that! Basically, the whole event just goes by very quickly and the next day you sort of feel like you want to do it all over again. I know we would have been annoyed with ourselves if we hadn't of captured the whole day professionally the way it was. We have some great pictures... and they all proved to be fab thank-you gifts for our relatives.'

chapter 14

The Honeymoon

These days when we talk of honeymoons, we often think of the 'honeymoon period', that first few giddy months of a relationship. The term honeymoon harks back to a golden past where even a kiss before marriage was considered risqué. It was the first time that a couple could truly be together and sleep together. The chances are that your honeymoon — should you choose to take one — is not going to be the first time you've ever shared a bed together. Some of you will have been together so long that it may seem unnecessary to take a honeymoon, others for just enough time to know that spending more than a few days alone in some far-flung five-star hotel will be enough to have you climbing the walls. Of course, this doesn't mean that you are not in love, just that you're not, well, in that honeymoon period anymore. But it would take a true cynic not to want to mark your civil partnership with some kind of quality time together, even if it's just for a night somewhere special.

As you've probably gathered by now, the theme of this book is to: make your own rules. If you think of the honeymoon as a special holiday, then that's probably what you'll get, at best. If you think about it as a chance — whatever your budget — to do something that you've both shared a passion for, or always wanted to do together, then there's a real opportunity to grab some of the profundity that is hinted at by the original meaning of honeymoon.

Whether it's lying on a tropical beach, jumping out of a plane at 10,000 ft or holing up in a gale-lashed fisherman's cottage somewhere near Aberdeen, both of you should think about what would be a perfect way to mark your honeymoon. Write this down. You may both have chosen the exact same villa on Gran Canaria, but probably you've come up with something different. Excellent: it's these kind of differences that attracted you to each other in the first place. Now you've got an opportunity to do something that combines and builds on these desires. Make sure you're in agreement and that you've got the budget and start planning. Yes, spontaneity is key to having a good time, and there should be plenty of room for ad-libbing wherever it is you go, but the golden rule to having a great holiday is sensible planning. We all know bad holiday experiences are a disappointment, but for a honeymoon it can be devastating.

WHERE TO GO

While it's unlikely that you've chosen distinctly gay-unfriendly Iran as your ideal honeymoon destination, there are many other places around the world, even within liberal countries, that won't be so quick to share your newly wed joy. If you're sure you just won't be able to keep your hands off each other in public, then maybe you should head for one of the world's 'gay Meccas' from London's Soho to Sydney's Oxford Street or San Francisco's Castro. A honeymoon partying in a queer capital will suit some just fine, others may find it all just a little bit unromantic; and if you're the jealous types, it might be wise to enjoy the tolerance of the location but stay off scene at night. There are, of course, plenty of other destinations worldwide where gay-friendly accommodation is easy to find, but where you can also escape the sex-charged atmosphere of the scene.

WHERE TO START

Traditionally, it's the job of the groom to organise and book the honeymoon. Well, that's not even going to get you to the airport, is it? Within your relationship, it's probable that one of you enjoys logistical tasks a little more than the other. If one of you wants to take the lead, fine. Just make sure the other is happy to help out where needed. Attempt as much as possible to split the costs, even if it means making sacrifices. The more you feel that this is your shared experience the stronger it is likely to be.

RESEARCH

Assuming you have both come up with some sort of happy compromise over the kind of honeymoon you want and roughly where to go, start thinking more carefully about what you want from your time away and find out everything you can about the destinations you are interested in. Read the guide books and magazines to get a feel for the atmosphere and facilities of the destination. It is ultimately a very personal decision, but communication and research is important to ensure you choose the honeymoon accommodation and resort that are right for you. One thing you'll have to think about is organising the time off from work, which will also force both of you to ask, 'How long does it to take to say "I Love You"?' A honeymoon time period ranges from a dirty weekend to a month's travelling the outback.

SAME-SEX HONEYMOON PACKAGES

As with wedding ceremonies, you can always buy a tailor-made honeymoon package. These can range from the very basic right up to the most extravagant, including safaris or even your own private plane to ferry you between destinations. Breathtaking views from some of the world's leading luxurious hotels have made European destinations like Italy appealing, as well as the romantic appeal of Venice and Verona. Among the more unusual destinations being offered now are rice boat cruises at Kerala on the southern tip of India and trips to Sri Lanka. But the average same-sex couple is likely to avoid the most predictable newly-wed destinations. Among the more diverse selections have been bookings to Vietnam.

HONEYMOON OPTIONS

Before you decide where you want to go, perhaps you should think about the overall style of honeymoon you want.

Surprise

Everyone loves surprises, but the implicit message of a surprise honeymoon is that the person making the plans is somehow the leader or breadwinner of the relationship. The obvious thing to plan here is a holiday you will both enjoy and to make sure that you have a good idea of your partner's expectations – then, basically, exceed them! Think about something your partner will really look forward to, and remember to let them know what sort of clothes to pack.

Relaxing

If all you want to do on your honeymoon is relax and spend some time together, then you should probably avoid the stress of long-haul flights. Why not try a cottage in the UK, which could serve you better than a gay resort in Ibiza?

Adventure

Your honeymoon could be an excuse to have a fabulous holiday together; if so, go for a bit of adventure. Whether it's an African safari, white-water rafting or trekking across the Himalayas, make sure you do thorough research before venturing out.

Sun, sea and sand

Walking hand-in-hand on a white, sandy beach is, to some, the high definition of a honeymoon. As long as you're not the type to get severely bored navel-gazing and pondering on the meaning of life whilst reading a Jackie Collins novel, a sweet and simple honeymoon will be a nice sunny resort.

Action

Walking, skiing, or rock climbing will sort out all the weight you've put on from having too much civil ceremony cake. If you've lasted this long in your relationship, there'll be no harm in registering for a bit of extreme sport action.

Road trip

Disappear into the sunset, or as close as British weather can offer, *Thelma & Louise* style. Although driving can be stressful, this holiday will secure a strong bond between you, alternating who sits in the passenger seat, who reads the map, who loses the keys, etc, etc.

Best of both worlds

For the unromantic and more realistic couple, find a holiday that caters for both of your needs. Popular choices nowadays consist of dual centre breaks, combining a week of beach-based relaxation with a more active or city-based week.

TOP EUROPEAN HONEYMOON DESTINATIONS

If you fancy a change of scene, but don't want to travel to the other end of the world, Europe has some fantastic cities that could be just what you're looking for.

Amsterdam

The heart of uninhibited Europe, Amsterdam is most famous for its canals, red light district and coffee-and-cannabis houses. Its laidback attitude means it is a youthful capital and a long-time favourite stage venue for the lads. Of course, it is also considered to be one of the most liberal cities for the gay community to enjoy. It has a large gay scene with hundreds of gay bars, discos, saunas, video stores, bookshops, restaurants and hotels. This is a honeymoon destination for a couple out for excitement rather than a quiet romance.

Dublin

Another classic stag destination with a high dosage of pubs offering the ultimate place to savour the tastiest pint of Guinness in the world. The city has its romantic and literary side too, Dublin has been home to some of the world's greatest writers, notably, Joyce, Shaw, Wilde and victim of unrequited love W B Yeats. Count yourselves lucky.

The gay scene is as friendly, playful and eccentric as you can imagine, starting south of the river with the Stonewall Café, a mixed but favoured gay venue. It's also a hotspot for practising homosexual vegetarians, with lots of New Age restaurants on offer. A hearty honeymoon for those who like a drink or two, or three or four.

Prague

Known as the 'Golden City of a Hundred Spires', Prague is a fairytale destination for a honeymoon crammed with romantic architecture. One of Europe's most beautifully preserved cities, its heart-stopping skyline is dominated by castle turrets, minarets and domes. The city is bisected by the swirling Vltava river and overlooked by seven hills, one of which is surmounted by Prague castle and its royal parks and gardens. It is small enough to wander around on foot, but there are always horse-drawn carriages for evening rides.

The first gay pride event was held just recently, but Prague has quite a large and well-developed gay and lesbian scene. A mix of romance and culture with a side-serving of gayness, Prague is a perfect honeymoon destination.

Ibiza

Already a favourite destination for the glam gays and lesbians who frequent Ibiza town's Calle de la Virgen, you'll find gay bars, gay restaurants, gay shops and a lot of overly tanned bodies. Ibiza is a prime location for same-sex honeymoons – particularly among same-sex party animals, presumably.

Ibiza is just a hop, skip and jump from other gay-friendly destinations, such as Barcelona and Palma. Ibiza town itself together with Figueretes, a suburb to the south of the city, forms the gay hub.

Reykjavik

This city is culturally very active, with a lively array of museums, cafés and music venues where you might even catch a glimpse of Björk. Alcohol is not cheap, but that doesn't stop the locals from getting absolutely wasted. There's not much in the way of a gay scene, but if that's not what you're after then Reykjavik is an ice cool honeymoon destination for those looking to escape the smell of amyl. And taking a bath in the steaming water of the geysers is high on anyone's romantic to-do lists.

If you're the type of modern gay couple looking to fit into a homogenous society, Iceland is the ideal, albeit expensive, honeymoon city. With a mere 300,000 Icelanders, you will receive a warm welcome. It's also ideal for a weekend break or shorter honeymoon, being a little under three hours from the UK.

Rome

If you're looking for a place that smashes the romance barometer look no further than Rome. History, culture, religion, style and cuisine, Rome has it all. With its ancient architecture making a perfect backdrop to your honeymoon snaps. You can even trot around on a Vespa with your partner packed on the back to really get in the spirit of the city.

You'll also be able to find a host of gay places to stay, eat, relax and party at, with quite an uninhibited selection of men's bars, most of them including showers, strippers and videos! Steer clear of this wrong side of Rome if you're going for the romance and not the smut.

 # AROUND THE WORLD

If you really want to push the boat out and make this a holiday to remember, here are some great suggestions that take you further afield.

Las Vegas

If you've already gone down the Elton John route on your civil partnership, you'd be wise to spend your honeymoon amid the bright lights of Las Vegas. This oasis of decadence and kitsch glamour is home to 19 of the 20 biggest hotels in the world; and let's face it, after the money you'll have blown on this shindig you'll be up for winning some money back in the casinos.

Bali

Known as the Island of the Gods, Bali has been a favourite haunt of Europeans looking for a cultured tropical island ever since it became a Mecca for artists in the 1930s. With a landscape of tropical rainforest, the island is studded with mystical shrines and Hindu temples and has a culture of traditional music and dance. It also has a thriving outdoor rave scene, with thumping beach parties never too far from the serenity.

New York

For those of you who can't get enough of the ghetto, what better way to spend a honeymoon than in the city that never sleeps. Offering round-the-clock entertainment, you and your partner will be overwhelmed by everything on offer, particularly if you've been before or know a good guide. Shopping at Fifth Avenue or cruising in Greenwich Village, it's all there for you!

Celebrity wedding

John and Jackie Kennedy made their honeymoon destination Acapulco world famous just for, well, going there. Choose an individual destination and start a trend of your own.

TRAVEL ADVICE

Depending on where you are jetting off to, there are always things to take into consideration, such as immunisation and vaccinations, and also countries with poor human rights records that would be particularly unsuitable for a same-sex honeymoon. You should also check that your destination is not going through any political or social upheaval at the time of travel and that there is no severe warning or disruption by natural disaster. If you are worried about a specific destination, the UK Government has a daily updated website to help advise you. See also other sources of travel info given on page 154.

BEFORE YOU GO

E-mail yourself

E-mail yourself all the important information: airline numbers, credit card phone numbers, passport and driving licence numbers. This way if your documents are lost or stolen, you will be able to access your missing details.

Tickets, money, passport!

Any way you want to remember it, these three vital things are all easily forgotten on your day of departure, especially when you're most probably still recovering from the party. If you forget everything else, it doesn't matter, so concentrate on the basics.

Travel insurance

Remember: travel operators will insist that you have cover before they'll send you on holiday. However, they cannot demand that you buy a policy from them, provided the cover you have is comparable. Apart from covering items that might be stolen while you're on holiday, including small amounts of cash, travel insurance offers many other important benefits. Policies usually include cover for medical expenses – useful if you fall ill or if you're unfortunate enough to be attacked and injured. You must disclose any pre-existing medical conditions.

If you're travelling within the EU, don't forget your European Health Insurance Card, which has replaced the old paper E111 form.

Travellers with chronic diseases

If your partner suffers from a chronic disease, or is HIV positive, certain circumstances, measures and limitations have to be taken into consideration.

All vital medication should be brought with you in your hand luggage, in sufficient quantities for the whole holiday, as experience has shown that your suitcase could end up somewhere completely different from where you actually land! Many countries have strict regulations on bringing medicine into the country, so a statement written by your GP saying that the medicine in question is vital and for your own exclusive use can ease your arrival. If it is a serious illness, such as HIV infection, you are unlikely to be able to obtain a pre-travel health statement; in connection with an ordinary insurance policy. You should think carefully about medical facilities in your chosen location and find out, for example, if a patient suffering from AIDS-related illness will be able to receive suitable respiratory care and medicines.

♥ top tips for insurance

- Always carry your insurance papers with you. Do not leave them where you are staying as you never know when you will need them!
- Always carry your identity papers on you. In many countries it's required by law.
- If you are allergic to any medications, put a note to that effect in with your identity papers. Don't assume you'll be conscious to give the doctor any details!
- Shop around ... and always read the small print of travel insurance, especially if you suffer from an existing medical condition.

♥ top tips for travelling

- Book early to get the honeymoon of your dreams. You're more likely to be offered a discount for an advance booking and you'll get the best choice of hotels.
- Ask your tour operator which airlines fly to your destination so you can compare prices and service. If you're going on a long-haul flight, find out which offer the best connections to make your journey as easy as possible.
- Check out the weather. You may have chosen your ideal location, but if it's going to be in the middle of the hurricane season...
- Don't be shy about letting everyone know it's your honeymoon. It's tradition for most places to offer you a gift of flowers or fruit, or to leave a bottle of champagne in your room on arrival.

VOX-POP

Max, 39, and Sebastian, 33, Henley-on-Thames

'Bringing on the tradition of a honeymoon for a civil union initially felt a bit silly. We'd been together for the last four years and already had fantastic holidays together. We opted for a long weekend away in Paris. We decided that the destination should at least be a romantic one, but then kept the duration of stay short so that we get back to our lives and got back to being normal, only this time as civil partners! With a honeymoon, it's really each to his or her own. I wouldn't discourage others to have a really long holiday, it just wasn't for us. We both definitely feel that a honeymoon, however long or short, is necessary, especially after all the stress incurred in the previous months!'

HONEYMOON CHECKLIST

Travel agent name	
Address	
Tel	
Fax	
E-mail	
Holiday dates	
Booking reference	
Departure date	
Departure time	
Depart from	
Destination	
Hotel/accommodation address	
Tel	
Fax	
E-mail	
Return date	
Return time	
Depart from	
Arrival time	
Arrive at	
Passport up to date	
Visas required	
Inoculations required	
Insurance	
Costs	
Deposit paid	
Date for receipt of tickets	

chapter 15

Love Is All There Is

'That Love is all there is, Is all we know of Love.' Emily Dickinson

So, civil partnership has arrived. What will the future bring now Britain has sat up, and taken notice of legally acknowledged LGBT unions? How will this impact on the gay community as a whole and change the way gay men and lesbians conduct relationships?

In the past, lesbians and gay men especially had to conduct their relationships in a covert manner. Homosexuality was illegal in Britain until 1967 and many homosexuals were unable to express publicly their natural thoughts and sexual desires, the great playwright Oscar Wilde being one such example. Even Queen Victoria did not acknowledge that such a phenomenon as 'lesbianism' existed. So haven't we come a long way!

Throughout the 1980s and 1990s, gay people gradually became more visible in society and gay scenes started to spring up, particularly in larger metropolitan areas. Homosexuals were increasingly able to be far more open about their relationships, and although there were sometimes cultural and religious dilemmas with being openly queer, the taboo and stigma of homosexuality was finally being dispelled.

But what could gay and lesbian couples really aspire to that involved legally recognised commitment, a union that was respected in government like heterosexual marriage? Of course, LGBT couples have been able to live together, and even adopt children together in recent times, but the opportunity of being able to spend a lifetime together hasn't pasted any legally binding glue or the cement of traditional marriage. Of course, civil partnership is not for everyone, in the same way that marriage is just a scrap of paper to some heterosexual partnerships; but it's all about having a legally recognised choice that society at large will acknowledge and respect. Of course, conservative religious and right-wing groups will be less forthcoming in accepting civil partnerships, but it would near impossible to wipe out pockets of homophobia with one piece of legislation, however progressive and pioneering it may be. However, at least with the Civil Partnership Act, the Government has passed something inherently positive and life-changing to reaffirm a belief that LGBT couples can, and will, make long-term commitments to one another.

But let's stop talking about all this formal business for a moment and talk about what's *really* important: love! Surely that is one of the main reasons why the majority of gay men and lesbians will be tying the knot in the foreseeable future. I think that this should be the primary reason why any couple chooses to get hitched. It may sound a little cheesy and contrived, but love is a beautiful, sacred entity and is a fundamental part of the ceremonial vernacular insomuch as you commit to cherishing and honouring your partner ''till death do you part' – scary prospect!

Of course, another crucial consideration is to protect each other's assets and to marry for financial means. While this is perfectly acceptable for couples looking to have economical peace of mind both today and tomorrow, I hope that civil partnership doesn't pave the way for marriages of convenience, i.e. a marriage entered into for expediency rather than love. After political groups like Stonewall have fought so hard to get us on level pegging with our heterosexual counterparts, why exploit civil partnerships and all that it stands for? Andy Forrest, the organisation's communications officer, has said, 'I think having civil partnerships is going to mean a lot more security, financially, without the need to seek legal recourse, which in turn means less stress and that will be beneficial.' So let's have less stress in our lives and show the country how stable, healthy gay relationships are an important aspect of contemporary society values. Let's keep those dissolution (divorce) rates down and show the sceptics how loyal and devoted we can be. And maybe even shift some stereotypes in the process too.

You should remember that by and large this book is about civil partnership, and although it is virtually the same as marriage in all but the name, it is different and we should embrace that distinction. We have the chance to really express ourselves, our values and our ways of life in an alternative marital environment. Throughout 2006, celebrations will mark some of the first civil partnerships in the country, and it will be fascinating to see how far and in which direction the market goes over the forthcoming years. Just as in any niche of society, the LGBT community will continue to evolve, grow and develop. We've gone from moustaches to mullets, dungarees to dykerama so who knows where the future of the gay community lies? With same-sex male and female couples having the option of a legally binding union, the community as we have known it will be forever changed and adapted, and this must surely be a positive step forward for each and every LGBT individual and their friends and family.

So, trip over love, you can get up. Fall in love and you fall forever. Make that commitment and show the world that civil partnership isn't a gloomy life sentence! Go on, it might just be one of the most important and rewarding decisions of your life.

Goodnight and good luck.

Contacts and Further Information

The Legalities

Jewish Gay and Lesbian Group

Support for Jewish gays, lesbians, bisexuals and their partners. Organises social, religious and informative events.
Address: BM JGLG, London WC1N 3XX
Tel: 020 8952 0137
info@jglg.org.uk
www.jglg.org.uk or

Liberal Judaism
www.liberaljudaism.org

Reform Judaism
www.reformjudaism.org.uk

Orthodox Judaism
www.unitedsynagogue.org.uk

LCGM (Lesbian and Gay Christians)
Oxford House, Derbyshire Street, London E2 6HG
Tel and Fax: 020 7739 1249
www.gcm.org.uk

Changing Attitude

A network of lesbian, gay, bisexual, transgender and heterosexual members of the Church of England.
12 Lavender Gardens, Battersea, London SW11 1DL
Tel: 020 7738 1305 Fax: 020 7738 0584
office@changingattitude.org.uk
www.changingattitude.org.uk

Imaan

PO Box 5369 London W1A 6SD
Tel: 07849 170793/07951 770735
info@imaan.org.uk
www.imaan.org.uk

UK Deed Poll

Freebournes Court, Witham, Essex CM8 2BL
www.deedpoll.org.uk

Stonewall

www.stonewall.org

Women & Equality Unit

www.womenandequalityunit.gov.uk/lgbt/partnership.htm

Home Office Immigration and Nationality Directorate

Tel: 0870 606 7766
www.ind.homeoffice.gov.uk

UK Lesbian and Gay Immigration Group

Tel: 020 7620 6010
www.uklgig.org.uk

Department for Work and Pensions

www.thepensionservice.gov.uk

HM Revenue and Customs

www.hmrc.gov.uk

Income-related benefits

www.jobcentreplus.gov.uk

General Register Office
www.gro.gov.uk

For specialist services
www.g3mag.co.uk
www.lynchlaw.co.uk
www.lorrells.com
www.russell-cooke.co.uk
www.martincray.co.uk

Just For You
Drag theme weddings
www.entsweb.co.uk/entertainers/drag/index.html

Wassup Pussycat ceremony package at the Gay Chapel of LV
1205 S. Las Vegas Blvd., 702-384-0771
Tel: +001 702-384-0771
www.gaychapeloflasvegas.com

Roaring '20s
Fantastic costumes based in London and Gatwick.
www.madworld-fancy-dress.co.uk

London Eye theme
Special Events Department, British Airways London Eye, Riverside
Building, County Hall, Westminster Bridge Road, London SE1 7PB
Tel: 0870 220 2223
Fax: 0870 990 8882
weddings@ba-londoneye.com
Web: www.ba-londoneye.com or www.lambeth.gov.uk

Other contacts for themed ceremonies
www.makeourday.co.uk
www.allnatt.co.uk
www.wedthemes.com
www.webwedding.co.uk/articles/weddingthemes/content.htm
www.weddinggazette.com/category/000723.shtml

General planning

www.weddingplanner.co.uk
www.pridebride.com
www.committed2pink.co.uk

The Stag and Hen Nights

www.berlin-tourist-information.de
www.amsterdam.info
www.iloveny.com
www.franceguide.com
www.partybus.co.uk

The Guests

www.Perfect-Wedding.org
www.weddinggoodies.co.uk
www.decadenceweddings.co.uk
www.funkyfairies.co.uk
www.peachcocktail.co.uk
www.lavenderlifestyles.co.uk

What To Wear

www.pinkproducts.co.uk
www.moderncommitments.co.uk
www.youandyourwedding.co.uk
www.weddingplanner.co.uk

Outlets for alternative clothes
www.cyberdog.net
Pioneering collection of cyberpunk garments on a global scale, with anything from LCD operated T-shirts to spiky PVC thongs.

www.madworld-fancy-dress.co.uk
Costumes as far ranging as traffic warden uniforms to movie star costumes such as Elvis or historical figures like King Arthur. Over 35,000 fancy dress costumes for hire from shops in central London and Gatwick.

www.clonezone.co.uk
One hundred per cent gay owned franchise located across the country selling a fantastic range of gay clothes and accessories.

www.avalonweddings.co.uk
Exclusive range of fantasy, period and gothic wedding gowns and accessories for weddings, handfastings and alternative ceremonies. All gowns and accessories are available in sizes 10 to 18 through mail order. In addition to its standard range, Avalon also provides a custom design service.

www.moonmaiden-gothic-clothing.co.uk
In the ancient, mystic depths of Celtic Cornwall, you will find some of the most romantic, dramatic gothic clothing you are liable to find online, including medieval gowns, wiccan robes and wonderful fishtail designs.

www.gothichaven.com
Gothic clothing, including garments for the voluptuous vamp, corsets, cyberwear, plus velvet, satin and gothic wedding and bridal wear.

The Ceremony
Buying a venue directory
Local Services, General Register Office, PO Box 56, Southport PR8 2GL
Tel: 0151 471 4817
local.services@ons.gov.uk

Jewellery
www.platinumringcompany.com
www.tiffany.com/uk
www.swarovski.com
www.stepheneinhorn.co.uk
www.aurumjewellers.com
www.bulgari.com

Other contacts
www.gay-friendly-wedding-venues.com

The Party
Catering
www.flyingchef.co.uk/canapes.html
www.tmkcatering.ie/menuideas/canapes.html
www.thepinkguide.co.uk
www.awesomecatering.com
www.creativecanapes.co.uk

Venues
www.place-recruitment.com
www.philpotsmanor.com
www.windmillhill.co.uk
www.scotland-inverness.co.uk/weddings.htm
www.tornacoille.com
www.pinkninetyone.co.uk

Entertainment
www.pink.prima-artists.com

The Speeches
www.famous-quotes-and-quotations.com/marriage-quotes.html
www.poets.org
www.rainbowsauce.com
www.gaysouthafrica.org.za/humour/male.asp

Capturing Your Memories
The Master Photographers' Association
www.thempa.com

British Institute of Professional Photography
www.bipp.com

The Honeymoon
Destinations
www.visitamsterdam.nl
www.queerid.com
Visitdublin.com
Praguegaycity.com
Prague-tourist-information.com
www.ibizaholidays.com
www.icelandtourist.is
www.gayrome.com
Romaturismo.com
www.fco.gov.uk

EHIC Applications
PO Box 1115, Newcastle upon Tyne, NE99 1SW
Tel: 0845 606 2030
www.ehic.org.uk

HM Revenue and Customs Centre for Non-Residents
Room BP1301, Benton Park View, Newcastle upon Tyne NE98 1ZZ
Tel: 0845 915 4811
www.dh.gov.uk

Department of Health Customer Service Centre
Room 320, Richmond House, 79 Whitehall, London SW1A 2NS
Tel: 020 7210 4850

Lesbian Travel Websites
Sappho Travel
Specialists in organising events and holidays for women to Greece and especially the island of Lesvos.
www.lesvos.co.uk

Rainbow Retreats
Lesbian/women only B&B in Andalucia, southern Spain.
www.womens-holiday.com

Lesvos Pride Tours
Accommodation, excursions, information and local support to gay and lesbian visitors to the Greek island of Lesvos.
www.lesvospridetours.com

Towanda
Women's motorcycling tours in New Zealand, Australia and California.
www.towanda.org

Lesbian b&b in Paris
Cosy rooms in the centre of Paris, French-style breakfast, all the info you need to know about the lesbian scene and Paris.
apinkfroggy@noos.fr

Casitas Laquita
Lesbian resort in Palm Springs, California, offering Romance Packages, as well as visits to the local golf course.
www.casitaslaquita.com

Gay travel websites
www.worldsforemost.com
www.pinkpassport.co.uk
www.rsvpvacations.com
www.gayresort.com

Index

A-line dresses 92
accessories
    for dresses 94–5
    for suits 88
accountability 18
affairs 17, 21
Amsterdam 138–39
Ancient Rome theme 43–4
arguments 16–17
attitudes
    family and friends 13, 69,
        103, 117
    of society 75, 145–46
    see also parents

Bali 141
ball gowns 90
bargain hunting 51
beach ceremonies 45
benefits, income-related 149
    joint assessment for 28, 29
'best man'
    speech 125–26
budgeting 47–57
    bargain hunting 51
    compulsory costs 51–2
    loans 49
    money saving tips 56
    sample budget sheets 53–5
    setting a budget 50–1
    stag nights 70–1
    sticking to the budget 52
    who pays? 47–8

cakes 110–11
    distributing 85
Camelot theme 44

caterers, choosing 109–10
catering 108–13
    checklist 112–13
ceremonies 31, 97–100
    guidelines 41–2
    names for 14
    personalising 99–100
    themed 41–5, 150
    timing 100
    venues 30, 52, 100, 102, 152
    wording of 31, 97–8
changes to relationships 20–2
children
    as guests 79, 108
    parenting 33
    responsibilities towards 28
    your own or your partners 17,
        28, 33
Christianity 35–6, 148–49
Civil Partnerships 9–13, 27,
    145–47
    advantages of 28
    comparisons with marriage
        9–10, 15–16, 26, 28
    dissolution of 32–3
    fees 30, 51–2
    frequently asked questions
        27–34
    giving notice 101–2
    history of the legislation
        11–13, 27–8
    and legal rights 10–11, 13, 28
    overseas registration of 32, 34
    pre-civil partnership
        agreements 33
    worldwide 26–7
    see also registration

clothes *see* outfits
cohabiting 20–1, 28, 30
column-style dresses 92
coming out 77
commitment 17–19
  life-long 15–16
  top tips 23
communication 22
  see also discussion
compatibility guide 24
confetti 114
costs *see* budgeting
cross-dressing 42, 87
  see also outfits

death of a partner 29
décor, reception 113–14, 115

deed polls 38–9, 149
differences, respecting 18–19
discussion
  about money 48
  before commitment 16–17,
    19, 21–2
dissolution 32–3
divorce procedure 32–3
double-barrelling surnames 38–9
drag theme 42, 150
dresses 89–93
drinks 111, 113
drugs at receptions 116
Dublin 139

e-mailing yourself honeymoon
  details 141
empire line dresses 91
entertainment 114–17, 153
ex-partners 70, 75

families 77, 78–9
  attitudes 13, 103, 117
  see also parents

fashion terms 90
'father of the bride' 124
favour boxes 85
fees 30, 51–2
flowers, reception 108, 113–14
forgiveness 22
friends 103–4
  non-gay 69
  stag and hen nights 69, 71

Gay Chapel of Las Vegas 43, 150
giving notice 101–2
goals, sharing 18–19
'groom's' speech 124–25
guests 100
  behaviour of 83–4
  children as 79, 108
  preparing list of 78–9
seating plans 107–8
  travelling 80

health *see* illness
hen nights *see* stag and hen
  nights
honesty 17
honeymoons 135–44, 154–55
  checklist 144
  e-mailing yourself details 141
  gay-friendly locations 136
  options 137–38
  same-sex packages 137
  top European destinations
    138–40
  top world destinations 140–41
  travel tips 141–43
Houston, Whitney 72
homophobia 146
  see also attitudes

Ibiza 139–40
illness
  and honeymoons 142

long-term 19
Imaan 36-7, 149
immigration 31, 101-2, 149
infidelity 17, 21
inheritance tax 29
insurance, travel 142, 143
intestacy rules 29
intolerance 13
    see also attitudes
invitations 81, 82, 84
Islam 36-7, 149

jealousy 21
jewellery 95, 152
John, Sir Elton 33, 74, 114
jokes 120-21
    see also pranks
Judaism 34-5, 148

Las Vegas 140
legal advice 30, 33
legal rights 10-11, 13, 28
legislation 10-11, 28
    history of 11-13, 27-8
licensed venues 30, 52, 100, 102,
    152
lighting for receptions 115
lingerie 95
living together 20-1, 28, 30
loans 49
London Eye ceremonies 45-6,
    150
lounge suits 89

marriage
    comparisons with 9-10,
        15-16, 26, 28
menu cards 85
mermaid and fishtail dresses 91-2
mini and midi style dresses 93
money
    loans 49

talking about 48
tips for saving 56
    see also budgeting
monogamy 15-16
morning suits 87-9
moving too fast 16, 20
music
    at the ceremony 98
    at the reception 115

name changes 32, 37-40
negotiation 22
    see also discussion
New York 141
notice of intention 31

O'Donnell, Rosie 34
open relationships 21-2
outfits 151-52
    alternative 95
    traditional for her (or him)
        89-95
    traditional for him (or her)
        87-9
overseas, partners from 31,
    101-2, 149
overseas registrations,
    recognition of 32, 34

parental responsibility 28, 33
parenting 17, 28, 33
parents
    financial support from 47, 48
    and guest lists 78-9
    and rehearsal dinners 81
    and stag nights 70
parties see receptions; stag and
    hen nights
partners
    children of 28, 33
    death of 29
    ex 70, 75

overseas 31, 101–2, 149
pension rights 29, 149
photographers
    amateur 130–31
    choosing professional 129–30
photographs 128–34, 153
    practising for 130
    sample checklists 131–32
pioneering 9–10, 22
Pitt, Brad 99
place cards 85
planning 150
    after the honeymoon 66
    big day 65–6
    countdown 58–65
    time of day 56
    time of year 51
Prague 139
pranks 72–3
    see also jokes
pre-civil partnership
    agreements 33
princess line dresses 91
privacy and registration
    addresses not published 31

quotations 127

receptions
    catering 108–13, 153
    décor 113–14, 115
    seating plans 107–8
    stationery 84–5
    time of day 104
    venues for 104–7, 153
registration
    addresses not published 31
    compulsory costs 30, 51–2
    notice of intention 31
    overseas 32, 34
    procedure 30
registration service 30

registry offices 30, 100, 150
rehearsal dinner invitations 81
relationships
    changes to 20–2
    commitment to 17–19
    monogamous 15–16
    moving too fast 16, 20
    open 21–2
religious ceremonies 10, 148–49
    prohibited during registration
        31, 99–100
    see also Christianity; Islam;
        Judaism
responsibilities 28
    sharing 21
    understanding 16
Reykjavik 140
rights, legal 10–11, 13, 28
rings, exchanging 98, 99
Roaring '20s theme 44–5, 150
Roberts, Julia 89
Rome 140

save-the-date cards 81
seating plans 107–8
self-catering 110
shoes 88, 94–5
society, attitudes of 75, 145–46
Spears, Britney 55
speeches 118–27, 153
    order of 123
    performing 123
    practising 122–23
    preparing 118–22
stag and hen nights 67–76, 151
    pranks 72–3
    themes and ideas 73–5
    together or alone? 68
    top tips 71, 75
    weekends 73
    who's in charge?
    whom to invite 69–70

stationery 44, 80–3
  personalised 84–5
step-children 33
suits 87–9
  for lesbian couples 93
surnames
  changing 32, 37–40
  double-barrelling 38–9

tax
  inheritance 29
  rights 29, 149
themes 41–5, 150
tiaras 94
timetable 58–66
travel
  advice 141
      insurance 142, 143

United States
  doesn't recognise civil
    partnerships 32

veils 94
venues
  licensed for registration 30,
    52, 100, 102, 152
  receptions 104–7, 153
videos 128
vows 97–8

Wassup Pussycat ceremony
  package 43
websites 148–55
  for photographs 129
wills, making 29
witnesses 99

Zellweger, Renee 83